Saul Bellow's Her-
zog

JE 16 92			
JE 9 04			

JAN '90

Modern Critical Interpretations

Saul Bellow's
Herzog

Modern Critical Interpretations

These and other titles in preparation

Saul Bellow's
Herzog

Edited and with an introduction by
Harold Bloom
Sterling Professor of the Humanities
Yale University

Chelsea House Publishers ◊ *1988*
NEW YORK ◊ NEW HAVEN ◊ PHILADELPHIA

© 1988 by Chelsea House Publishers, a division
of Chelsea House Educational Communications, Inc.,
   95 Madison Avenue, New York, NY 10016
   345 Whitney Avenue, New Haven, CT 06511
   5068B West Chester Pike, Edgemont, PA 19028

Introduction © 1986 by Harold Bloom

Printed and bound in the United States of America

10 9 8 7 6 5 4 3 2 1

∞ The paper used in this publication meets the minimum
requirements of the American National Standard for
Permanence of Paper for Printed Library Materials, Z39.48–
1984.

Library of Congress Cataloging-in-Publication Data
Saul Bellow's Herzog.
   (Modern critical interpretations)
   Bibliography: p.
   Includes index.
   1. Bellow, Saul.   Herzog. I. Bloom, Harold.
II. Series.
PS3503.E4488H49   1988   813′.52   87-23924
ISBN 1-55546-059-3 (alk. paper)

Contents

Editor's Note

This book brings together a representative selection of the best critical interpretations of Saul Bellow's novel *Herzog*. The critical essays are reprinted here in the chronological order of their original publication. I am grateful to Donna Stowe and Paul Barickman for their assistance in editing this volume.

My introduction sets *Herzog* in the context of Bellow's career, with its long polemic against literary modernism, and its related nostalgia for Jewish normative tradition. The chronological sequence of criticism begins with Tony Tanner's appreciation, which accepts Moses Herzog as the modern mind laboring with the burden of ideas.

Gabriel Josipovici charts the passage of Herzog, who rejects both "crisis ethics" and "potato love," and instead accepts responsibility for himself. In Sarah Blacher Cohen's view, Herzog surmounts egotism and achieves community through his resilient wit.

In a dissenting judgment, Richard Poirier discovers an unfortunate complicity in the self-aggrandizing cultural stances of Herzog and of Bellow. Far more Bellovian, Daniel Fuchs joins Bellow in *Herzog*'s humanist critique of what Bellow insists upon regarding as Freud's severity and rigidity on the issues of psychic over-determination.

In a defense of Madeleine Herzog's character, Ada Aharoni argues that Madeleine is the psychic center both of Herzog's existence and of the novel. Jonathan Wilson, in this volume's final essay, locates the novel's "deep subject" as Herzog's sense of ambivalent manhood because of his position as an intellectual in a society that defines masculine reality in terms of business and politics. This accounts (according to Wilson) for the paradox that Herzog becomes healthier at the expense of part of his intellectual vitality.

Introduction

By general critical agreement, Saul Bellow is the strongest American novelist of his generation, presumably with Norman Mailer as his nearest rival. What makes this canonical judgment a touch problematic is that the indisputable achievement does not appear to reside in any single book. Bellow's principal works are: *The Adventures of Augie March, Herzog, Humboldt's Gift,* and in a briefer compass, *Seize the Day.* The earlier novels, *Dangling Man* and *The Victim*, seem now to be period pieces, while *Henderson the Rain King* and *Mr. Sammler's Planet* share the curious quality of not being quite worthy of two figures so memorable as Henderson and Mr. Sammler. *The Dean's December* is a drab book, its dreariness unredeemed by Bellow's nearly absent comic genius.

Herzog, still possessing the exuberance of *Augie March*, while anticipating the tragicomic sophistication of *Humboldt's Gift*, as of now seems to be Bellow's best and most representative novel. And yet its central figure remains a wavering representation, compared to some of the subsidiary male characters, and its women seem the wish-fulfillments, negative as well as positive, of Herzog and his creator. This seems true of almost all of Bellow's fiction: a Dickensian gusto animates a fabulous array of secondary and minor personalities, while at the center a colorful but shadowy consciousness is hedged in by women who do not persuade us, though evidently once they persuaded him.

In some sense, the canonical status of Bellow is already assured, even if the indubitable book is still to come. Bellow's strengths may not have come together to form a masterwork, but he is hardly the first novelist of real eminence whose books may be weaker as aggregates than in their component parts or aspects. His stylistic achievement is beyond dispute, as are his humor, his narrative inventiveness, and his astonishing inner ear, whether for monologue or dialogue. Perhaps his greatest gift is for creating subsidiary and minor characters of grotesque splendor, sublime in their vivacity, intensity, and capacity to surprise. They may be caricatures, yet their vitality seems permanent: Einhorn, Clem Tembow, Bateshaw, Valentine Gersbach, Sandor Himmelstein, Von Humboldt Fleisher, Cantabile, Alec Szathmar. Alas, compared to them, the narrator-heroes, Augie, Herzog, and Citrine, are diffuse beings, possibly because Bellow cannot disengage from them, despite heroic efforts and revisions. I remember *Augie March* for Einhorn, *Herzog* for Gersbach, *Humboldt's Gift* for Humboldt, and even that last preference tends to throw off-center an apprehension of the novel. Augie March and Herzog narrate and speak with tang and eloquence, yet they themselves are less memorable than what they say. Citrine, more subdued in his language, fades yet more quickly into the continuum of Bellow's urban cosmos. This helps compound the aesthetic mystery of Bellow's achievement. His heroes are superb observers, worthy of their Whitmanian heritage. What they lack is Whitman's Real Me or Me Myself, or else they are blocked from expressing it.

II

Few novelists have ever surpassed Bellow at openings and closings:

> I am an American, Chicago born—Chicago, that somber city—and go at things as I have taught myself, free-style, and will make the record in my own way: first to knock, first admitted; sometimes an innocent knock, sometimes a not so innocent. But a man's character is his fate, says Heraclitus, and in the end there isn't any way to disguise the nature of the knocks by acoustical work on the door or gloving the knuckles.

> Look at me, going everywhere! Why, I am a sort of Columbus of those near-at-hand and believe you come to them in this immediate *terra incognita* that spreads out in every gaze. I may well be a flop at this line of endeavor. Columbus too thought he was a flop, probably, when they sent him back in chains. Which didn't prove there was no America.

The end and the start cunningly interlace, very much in the mode of *Song of Myself,* or of the first and last chapters of Emerson's *Nature.* Augie too is an American Transcendentalist, a picaresque quester for the god within the self. *Ethos* is the *Daimon*, both passages say, with Augie as ethos and Columbus as the daimon. One remembers the aged Whitman's self-identification in his "Prayer of Columbus," and it seems right to rejoice, as Whitman would have rejoiced, when Augie comes full circle from going at things, self-taught and free-style, to discovering those near-at-hand, upon the shores of America. That is Bellow at his most exuberant. When weathered, the exuberance remains, but lies in shadow:

> If I am out of my mind, it's all right with me, thought Moses Herzog.
>
> Some people thought he was cracked and for a time he himself had doubted that he was all there. But now, though he still behaved oddly, he felt confident, cheerful, clairvoyant, and strong. He had fallen under a spell and was writing letters to everyone under the sun. . . . Hidden in the country, he wrote endlessly, fanatically, to the newspapers, to people in public life, to friends and relatives and at last to the dead, his own obscure dead, and finally the famous dead.

> Perhaps he'd stop writing letters. Yes, that was what was coming, in fact. The knowledge that he was done with these letters. Whatever had come over him during these last months, the spell, really seemed to be passing, really going. He set down his hat, with the roses and day lilies, on the half-painted piano, and went into his study, carrying the wine bottles in one hand like a pair of Indian clubs. Walking over notes and papers, he lay down on his Récamier couch. As he stretched out, he took a long breath, and then he lay, looking at the mesh of the screen, pulled loose by vines, and listening to the steady scratching of Mrs. Tuttle's broom. He wanted to tell her to sprinkle the floor. She was raising too much dust. In a few minutes he would call down to her, "Damp it down, Mrs. Tuttle. There's water in the sink." But not just yet. At this time he had no messages for anyone. Nothing. Not a single word.

Another *ritorno,* but this time the cycle has been broken. Augie March, like Emerson and Whitman, knows that there is no history, only biography. Moses Herzog has been a long time discovering this truth, which ends his profession, and Charlie Citrine also goes full-circle:

The book of ballads published by Von Humboldt Fleisher in the Thirties was an immediate hit. Humboldt was just what everyone had been waiting for. Out in the Midwest I had certainly been waiting eagerly, I can tell you that. An avant-garde writer, the first of a new generation, he was handsome, fair, large, serious, witty, he was learned. The guy had it all. All the papers reviewed his book. His picture appeared in *Time* without insult and in *Newsweek* with praise. I read *Harlequin Ballads* enthusiastically. I was a student at the University of Wisconsin and thought about nothing but literature day and night. Humboldt revealed to me new ways of doing things. I was ecstatic. I envied his luck, his talent, and his fame, and I went east in May to have a look at him—perhaps to get next to him. The Greyhound bus, taking the Scranton route, made the trip in about fifty hours. That didn't matter. The bus windows were open. I had never seen real mountains before. Trees were budding. It was like Beethoven's *Pastorale*. I felt showered by the green, within . . . Humboldt was very kind. He introduced me to people in the Village and got me books to review. I always loved him.

Within the grave was an open concrete case. The coffins went down and then the yellow machine moved forward and the little crane, making a throaty whir, picked up a concrete slab and laid it atop the concrete case. So the coffin was enclosed and the soil did not come directly upon it. But then, how did one get out? One didn't, didn't, didn't! You stayed, you stayed! There was a dry light grating as of crockery when contact was made, a sort of sugarbowl sound. Thus, the condensation of collective intelligences and combined ingenuities, its cables silently spinning, dealt with the individual poet. . . .

Menasha and I went toward the limousine. The side of his foot brushed away some of last autumn's leaves and he said, looking through his goggles, "What this, Charlie, a spring flower?"

"It is. I guess it's going to happen after all. On a warm day like this everything looks ten times deader."

"So it's a little flower," Menasha said. "They used to tell one about a kid asking his grumpy old man when they were walking in the park, 'What's the name of this flower, Papa?' and the old guy is peevish and he yells, 'How should I know? Am I in the millinery business?' Here's another, but what do you suppose they're called, Charlie?"

"Search me," I said. "I'm a city boy myself. They must be crocuses."

The cycle is from Citrine's early: "I felt showered by the green, within" to his late, toneless, "They must be crocuses," removed from all affect not because he has stopped loving Humboldt, but because he is chilled preternaturally by the effective if unfair trope Bellow has found for the workings of canonical criticism: "Thus, the condensation of collective intelligences and combined ingenuities, its cables silently spinning, dealt with the individual poet." There is no history, and now there is also no biography, but only the terrible dehumanizing machine of a technocratic intelligentsia, destroying individuality and poetry, and stealing from the spring of the year the green that no longer is to be internalized.

III

Bellow's endless war against each fresh wave of literary and intellectual modernism is both an aesthetic resource and an aesthetic liability in his fiction. As resource, it becomes a drive for an older freedom, an energy of humane protest against over-determination. As liability, it threatens to become repetition, or a merely personal bitterness, even blending into Bellow's acerbic judgments upon the psychology of women. When it is most adroitly balanced, in *Herzog*, the polemic against modernism embraces the subtle infiltrations of dubious ideologies into the protesting Moses Herzog himself. When it is least balanced, we receive the narrative rant that intrudes into Mr. Sammler's cosmos, or the dankness that pervades both Chicago and Bucharest in *The Dean's December*. Like Ruskin lamenting that the water in Lake Como was no longer blue, Bellow's Alexander Corde tells us that "Chicago wasn't Chicago anymore." What *The Dean's December* truly tells us is that "Bellow wasn't Bellow anymore," in this book anyway. The creator of Einhorn and Gersbach and Von Humboldt Fleisher gives us no such figure this time around, almost as though momentarily he resents his own genius for the high comedy of the grotesque.

Yet Bellow's lifelong polemic against the aestheticism of Flaubert and his followers is itself the exuberant myth that made *Augie March, Herzog,* and *Humboldt's Gift* possible. In an act of critical shrewdness, Bellow once associated his mode of anti-modernist comedy with Svevo's *Confessions of*

Zeno and Nabokov's *Lolita*, two masterpieces of ironic parody that actually surpass Bellow's *Henderson the Rain King* in portraying the modernist consciousness as stand-up comic. Parody tends to negate outrage, and Bellow is too vigorous to be comfortable at masking his own outrage. When restrained, Bellow is too visibly restrained, unlike the mordant Svevo or the Nabokov who excels at deadpan mockery. Henderson may be more of a self-portrait, but Herzog, scholar of High Romanticism, better conveys Bellow's vitalistic version of an anti-modernistic comic stance. Bellow is closest to Svevo and to Nabokov in the grand parody of Herzog-Hamlet declining to shoot Gersbach-Claudius when he finds the outrageous adulterer scouring the bathtub after bathing Herzog's little daughter. Daniel Fuchs, certainly Bellow's most careful and informed scholar, reads this scene rather too idealistically by evading the parodic implications of "Moses might have killed him now." Bathing a child is our sentimental version of prayer, and poor Herzog, unlike Hamlet, *is* a sentimentalist, rather than a triumphant rejecter of nihilism, as Fuchs insists.

Bellow, though carefully distanced from Herzog, is himself something of a sentimentalist, which in itself need not be an aesthetic disability for a novelist. Witness Samuel Richardson and Dickens, but their sentimentalism is so titanic as to become something different in kind, a sensibility of excess larger than even Bellow can hope to display. In seeking to oppose an earlier Romanticism (Blake, Wordsworth, Whitman) to the belated Romanticism of literary modernism (Gide, Eliot, Hemingway), Bellow had the peculiar difficulty of needing to avoid the heroic vitalism that he regards as an involuntary parody of High Romanticism (Rimbaud, D. H. Lawrence, and, in a lesser register, Norman Mailer). Henderson, Bellow's Gentile surrogate, is representative of just how that difficulty constricts Bellow's imagination. The Blakean dialectic of Innocence and Experience, clearly overt in the scheme of the novel, is at odds with Henderson's characteristically Bellovian need for punishment or unconscious sense of guilt, which prevails in spite of Bellow's attempts to evade Freudian overdetermination. Though he wants and indeed needs a psychology of the will, Bellow is much more Freudian than he can bear to know. Henderson is a superbly regressive personality, very much at one with the orphan child he holds at the end of the novel. Dahfu, of whom Norman Mailer strongly approved, is about as persuasive a representation as are his opposites in Bellow, all of those sadistic and compelling fatal ladies, pipe dreams of a male vision of otherness as a castrating force. Bellow disdains apocalypse as a mode, but perhaps the Bellovian apocalypse would be one in which all of the darkly attractive women of these novels converged upon poor Dahfu, Blakean vitalist, and divested him of the emblem of his therapeutic vitalism.

Without his polemic, Bellow never seems able to get started, even in *Humboldt's Gift*, where the comedy is purest. Unfortunately, Bellow cannot match the modernist masters of the novel. In American fiction, his chronological location between, say, Faulkner and Pynchon exposes him to comparisons he does not seek yet also cannot sustain. Literary polemic within a novel is dangerous because it directs the critical reader into the areas where canonical judgments must be made, as part of the legitimate activity of reading. Bellow's polemic is normative, almost Judaic in its moral emphases, its passions for justice and for more life. The polemic sometimes becomes more attractive than its aesthetic embodiments. Would we be so charmed by Herzog if he did not speak for so many of us? I become wary when someone tells me that she or he "loves" *Gravity's Rainbow*. The grand Pynchonian doctrine of sado-anarchism scarcely should evoke *affection* in anyone, as opposed to the shudder of recognition that the book's extraordinary aesthetic dignity demands from us. It is the *aesthetic* failure of Bellow's polemic, oddly combined with its moral success, that increasingly drives Bellow's central figures into dubious mysticisms. Citrine's devotion to Rudolf Steiner is rather less impressive, intellectually and aesthetically, than the obsessive Kabbalism of *Gravity's Rainbow*. If Steiner is the ultimate answer to literary modernism, then Flaubert may rest easy in his tomb.

IV

And yet Bellow remains a humane comic novelist of superb gifts, almost unique in American fiction since Mark Twain. I give the last words here to what moves me as the most beautiful sequence in Bellow, Herzog's final week of letters, starting with his triumphant overcoming of his obsession with Madeleine and Gersbach. On his betraying wife, Herzog is content to end with a celebration now at last beyond masochism: "To put on lipstick, after dinner in a restaurant, she would look at her reflection in a knife blade. He recalled this with delight." On Gersbach, with his indubitable, latently homosexual need to cuckold his best friend, Herzog is just and definitive: "*Enjoy her—rejoice in her. You will not reach me through her, however, I know you sought me in her flesh. But I am no longer there.*" The unmailed messages go on, generously assuring Nietzsche of Herzog's admiration while telling the philosopher: "*Your immoralists also eat meat. They ride the bus. They are only the most bus-sick travelers.*" The sequence magnificently includes an epistle to Dr. Morgenfruh, doubtless a Yiddish version of the Nietzschean Dawn of Day, of whom Herzog wisely remarks: "He was a splendid old man, only partly fraudulent, and what more can you ask of anyone?" Addressing Dr. Morgenfruh, Herzog speculates darkly "that the territorial instinct is stronger than the sexual." But then, with exquisite grace, Herzog signs off: "*Abide in light, Morgenfruh. I will keep you posted from time to time.*" This benign farewell is made not by an over-determined bundle of territorial and sexual instincts, but by a persuasive representative of the oldest ongoing Western tradition of moral wisdom and familial compassion.

The Prisoner of Perception

Tony Tanner

> *His face was before him in the blotchy mirror. It was bearded with*
> *lather. He saw his perplexed, furious eyes and he gave an audible cry.*
> My God! Who is this creature? It considers itself human. But
> what is it? Not human of itself. But has the longing to be
> human.

This is Moses E. Herzog, the central figure in Bellow's most recent novel,
entitled *Herzog*. (His name almost certainly derives from Joyce's *Ulysses*
where there is a minor character called Moses Herzog who is a put-upon
Jewish merchant. It may also contain a distant reference to the famous and
very brave mountaineer, Maurice Herzog.) This book—Bellow's most impressive to this date—seems to summarise and contain all the questions,
the problems, the feelings, the plights, and the aspirations worked over in
the previous novels, and it follows them out to their extremest reaches. It
seems to be the result of a conclusive grappling with the gathering preoc-
cupations of years. Herzog himself is clearly a descendant, if not a summa-
tion, of Bellow's other main characters—worried, harassed, brought
down, messed up. His private life is at a point of chaos—for he is trying
to recover from a disastrous second marriage which has just ended in divorce. He is condemned to perpetual compulsive introspection, the victim
of memories which refuse to be shut out, racked by endless, nagging cerebration. He seems terribly isolated and cut-off, wandering the congested
city streets, brooding apart in lonely rooms. The book contains few actual

From *Saul Bellow*. © 1965 by Tony Tanner. Barnes & Noble Books, Totowa,
New Jersey, 1965.

9

incidents in the present—an abortive trip to Vineyard Haven, a night with a girl friend, a visit to Chicago to see one of his children which ends with a car crash, the return to an old tumble-down house in the country which was where his second marriage reached its ultimate crisis. The significant action mainly takes part in his head. People and incidents teem through his memory, precipitating great bouts of agitated soul-searching and pounding speculation. More than that, his mind heaves under the weight and pressure, not only of his personal worries, but of the modern city, the innumerable problems of the modern age; ultimately it finds itself struggling with the deepest questions and mysteries of Man himself. His mind seems compelled to take on itself the burden of the whole world, the problem of mankind; yet as a physical being his relationships are fouled up, he is separated from his children, he is one of the struggling sweating mass—powerless, something of a failure, not a little lost. Yet his mind will not be stilled. There is irony as well as urgency in his predicament and Bellow excels himself in this book by presenting not only the importance, but also the curse and the comedy of intense consciousness. Herzog's is a representative modern mind, swamped with ideas, metaphysics and values, and surrounded by messy facts. It labours to cope with them all. The book enacts that labour.

At first sight, the meaning of the book might seem to be the sum of all the dozens of ideas that course through Herzog's mind. Yet a more careful view reveals a deeper, subtler intent. The book moves from a corrosive restlessness to a point of temporary rest, and the most important meaning is in that actual movement: the internal labour finally gives way to a glimpse of peace. A consideration of the form and technique of the book can help us to understand this better. A brief opening passage shows us a "tranquil" Herzog, alone in his old country house during the "peak of summer." Then it takes us back to the start of all his troubles. "Late in spring Herzog had been overcome by the need to explain, to have it out, to justify, to put in perspective, to clarify, to make amends." This compulsion to *understand*—typical of Bellow's protagonists—manifests itself in Herzog's habit of making endless notes and jottings, recording fragmentary thoughts, and observations. More than that he gets into the habit of writing letters—to friends, relations, dead ancestors, politicians, philosophers, finally even to God. Many of them are unfinished, none of them, as far as we know, are ever sent. Perhaps they are all imaginary, part of his internal continuum, sudden moments of excited hyperconsciousness when the mind engages in silent partnerless dialogues—"having it out," trying to clarify. Meanwhile Herzog is often sitting or lying down, "in the coop of his privacy." For the bulk of the book we are in that coop with him—going over things, witnesses of this endless, silent self-examination. It is not systematic: like his life it is mismanaged and patternless. He cannot organise the mixed swarm of facts, notions and ideas: "consciousness when it doesn't clearly understand what to live for, what to die for, can only abuse and ridicule itself." For much of the book Herzog suffers from "unemployed consciousness."

The book has to bring us not only the excitement of the ideas, but the strain, the futility, the near insanity which Herzog experiences. So the reminiscences and the thoughts and the letters flow, one into the other, like a troubled stream. There are sudden interruptions, extremely vivid, graphic evocations of New York or Chicago—unrelated, sudden heightenings of external pressure. The harsh noise and density of the city seem only to drive Herzog deeper into himself. He is never more lost in thought than on the subway. Significant human contact is minimal; even with Ramona, his current girlfriend, he seems ultimately detached, only intermittently stimulated to a brief sexual activity accompanied by a little incipient emotion. He can recall many affairs; he loves his brothers and children; he has long talks with certain friends. But for the most part he seems quite incapable of any genuine relationships. His memory is densely populated—yet he moves like a solitary, sealed up in himself, ridden by a million thoughts. Writing letters to the void, while reality ebbs away from him.

But a counter-movement grows increasingly strong—a desire to reengage simple reality, a yearning for a reprieve from this excess of solitary cerebration, a desire to pass beyond the impossible task of mental justification. His first instinct had been to explain. By the end he is meditating:

> *A curious result of the increase of historical consciousness is that people think explanation is a necessity of survival. They have to explain their condition. And if the unexplained life is not worth living, the explained life is unbearable, too.*

The book follows out his doomed attempts to explain and synthesise until we can feel with Herzog the need and the possibility for some new commencement and calm somewhere on the other side of "explanation." At the end Herzog is tranquil in his country house—as we glimpsed him at the start. Now we understand that tranquillity. But only because we have experienced to the full the turmoil which preceded it.

We shall have to look more closely at some of the ideas that Herzog wrestles with for they are crucial ideas in Bellow's work. But it must first be emphasised that Herzog is in no normal state: it is part of the meaning of the book that these ideas are being turned over by a mind in the throes of a riot of subjectivism. He is often in the state he finds himself enduring in Grand Central Station "both visionary and muddy . . . feverish, damaged, angry, quarrelsome, and shaky." On a train he will start various letters to people as various as Adlai Stevenson, Ramona, Nehru, Commissioner Wilson—and himself. His reaction at the time is typical:

> Quickly, quickly, more! . . . Herzog now barely looking through the tinted, immovable, sealed window felt his eager, flying spirit streaming out, speaking, piercing, making clear judgments, uttering final explanations, necessary words only. He was in a whirling ecstasy. He felt at the same time that his judgments exposed the boundless, baseless bossiness and wilfulness, the nagging embodied in his mental constitution.

The sealed window—the soaring mind: the certainty as to the importance of his thoughts—a suspicion that they result from a ridiculous tantrum. That is typical Herzog. He cannot select or filter his thoughts. "I am a prisoner of perception, a compulsory witness." This is a mind with no certainties, no calm programme, no sure focus. A mind in pain. "He wrote to Spinoza. *Thoughts not causally connected were said by you to cause pain. I find that is indeed the case. Random association, when the intellect is passive, is a form of bondage.*"

Like many another alienated observer, he wonders if anguish and detachment are the necessary condition of his calling. "Moses had to see reality. Perhaps he was somewhat spared from it so that he might see it better, not fall asleep in its thick embrace. Awareness was his work; extended consciousness was his line, his business. Vigilance." Looking at his brother, a man immersed in business, Herzog contrasts himself—"a man like me has shown the arbitrary withdrawal of proud subjectivity from the collective and historical progress of mankind." But he says this in self-mockery, and by the end he drops the idea as a vain-glorious falsehood. Gradually, the prisoner starts to emerge. Here is a crucial moment after a heavy spell of speculation and vast generalisations:

> But then he realized that he did not need to perform elaborate abstract intellectual work—work he had always thrown himself into as if it were the struggle for survival. But not thinking is not necessarily fatal. Did I really believe that I would die when thinking stopped?

(Herzog alternates between addressing himself as "I" and "he," and even "you"; while not completely schizophrenic, it does suggest mental disturbance as well as comic detachment.) The habit of subjectivism, explanation, thought itself, becomes almost a plague, a genuine neurosis, of which he is at least partially cured by the end of the book as he moves towards reality's "thick embrace."

But his self-communings and memories compromise the bulk of the book. True, the city-scapes are incomparably vivid, detailed, and pungent; essentially *there* so we can really feel the background against which the modern mind works, and has to work. Herzog feels part of the New York mess, and indeed there seems to be at times an intimate connexion between the city and his thoughts. Perhaps the teeming confusion of its chaos agitates his mind into a state of overexcited emulation—the city triggering off the spasms of unrelated thoughts, just as the thoughts sometimes grind to an inconclusive halt in the congestion of the city streets. Thus in Chicago: "He was perhaps as midwestern and unfocused as these same streets. Not so much determinism, he thought, as lack of determining elements—the absence of a formative power." For all that, the most important reality in the book is inside Herzog's head, in the ramifications of his ungovernable memory and the fretful reachings of his mind. It is there that we meet most of the characters in his life, and relive some of his most intense experiences. It is there that Herzog establishes contact with his ancestors and reenacts his "ancient times." As though he is trying to form some sort of community in his head to compensate for the absence of it in society at large. It is part of his effort to "make steady progress from disorder to harmony," to capture a sense of lineage out of the welter of the past—the past of Moses Herzog, of his family, his race, his culture, Man himself. Many of his letters are to the dead. "But then why shouldn't he write the dead? He lived with them as much as with the living—perhaps more." He knows what an "insidious blight" nostalgia is, but his prolonged excursions into the past are only partially self-indulgence and escapism. For it is in his memory that Herzog is seeking some lost reality, some necessary key which will help him to align himself with the norms from which he has wandered and blundered into his personal chaos and separation. He must expose himself to everything, excluding nothing (not even the traumatic sexual assault he suffered as a child) before he can learn true acceptance and a new orientation. Mental regurgitation is part of his therapy: the way back to a point at which life can be resumed lies through memory. "Engrossed, unmoving in his chair, Herzog listened to the dead at their dead quarrels." Some of the most powerful and moving scenes are of his family, his youth, the sufferings of his "late unlucky father": scenes and characters are re-created with an astonishing and compelling wealth of circumstantial detail, while Herzog seems to go into a sort of catatonic trance, engulfed by the past.

Note that Bellow is not concerned to give a straightforward, chronological biography of Herzog. He is concerned to show a middle-aged confused man beset by teeming fragments of the past, trying to relate them, seeking coherence, trying to disentangle from them all some sense of necessary ancestry, and stabilising orientation. Similarly with the characters and events of Herzog's own adult life—they are recalled, summoned up in love or anger, or allowed to drift in and out of the periphery of his mind. There are well over a score of characters, who loom into focus with extreme individual vividness—his wives, his women, psychiatrists, lawyers, fellow academics, brothers, writers, childhood friends, as well as his parents and older relations. Inevitably many of the incidents he recalls with these people are essentially conversations, discussions, disagreements, rows. Apart from sex, and some travel, most of Herzog's more recent experience has been mainly verbal. This indeed, is perhaps part of the disease—his own, his age's. "People legislate continually by means of talk." Like Augie, Herzog is surrounded by people who want to give him advice, manipulate him, impose their view of things, their realities, on his. Some of them—his second wife, her lover, her lawyer—actually plot against him for his money, and his children, but most of the pressures are verbal. Augie found himself surrounded by Machiavellians: Herzog is set down among "Reality Instructors"—people who positively enjoy thrusting forward the low view of truth, cruel in their relish of the nastiness of life. And even Moses himself recognises that he, too, wants to teach his ideas. "*A very special sort of lunatic expects to inculcate his principles.* Sandor Himmelstein, Valentine Gersbach, Madeleine P. Herzog, Moses himself. *Reality Instructors. They want to teach you—to punish you with—the lessons of the Real.*" But one question abides with Herzog which he silently puts to the world of Reality Instructors. "*What makes you think realism must be brutal?*" Part of his quest is for a higher view which nevertheless does not blink the brutality which is undoubtedly there.

Herzog recalls people and incidents as often as not because he wishes to take issue with their views, or consider the implications of their acts. We get very little external reality straight—indeed it is possible that the whole book is a reminiscence. (There is a slight, perhaps deliberate ambiguity, about the time lapse between the start and the end. One is not sure whether something is actually taking place or being remembered. Indeed, it is possible that Herzog is remembering previous memories. The book ends where it began.) Situations, characters, and events for the most part come to us coloured by his memory, penetrated by his questioning: often broken up or interrupted by a burst of letter-writing. Herzog calls his letter-writing and scribbling of odd notes "ridiculous," but he falls into it continually. Some of the letters are comic, some angry, some desperate, some urgent, many of them theoretical and pedagogic. They are a way of relieving the accumulating pressures on his mind; also they are part of his vast attempt to take stock, understand, and clarify. Into them he puts his needs, his resentments, his quarrels with the creeds of his age; through them he expresses his inchoate beliefs and tentative faith. Perhaps also they not only help him to come to terms with the dizzying clutter of his life and times, but also serve as a means whereby he can disburden himself of that clutter. But as a phenomenon, irrespective of what Herzog writes in them, these letters and notes are symptoms of a plight and desire which are basic in Bellow's work. Herzog says to himself, in words which remind us of so many other Bellow protagonists: "I seem to have been stirred fiercely by a desire to communicate, or by the curious project of attempted communication." All those prolific letters simply serve to emphasise Herzog's silence, his basic isolation and apartness and indrawnness. He carries the world in his head. But the desire to communicate is real and points the way to a possible redemption from a habit of introspection which could lead to solipsism.

Herzog's thoughts and concerns are too various to summarise; indeed their profuse, unrelated multiplicity is an essential part of the meaning of the book. But a few concerns which have always seriously engaged Bellow recur, and Herzog wrestles with problems and ideas that other characters in Bellow's work have also attacked and pondered, and that Bellow himself has discussed in many articles. Some of these should be mentioned. For instance Herzog returns continually to the question of the value and importance of the individual self. The great work he was meditating before he started to go to pieces was going to show "how life could be lived by renewing universal connections; overturning the last of the Romantic errors about the uniqueness of the Self," and he thinks back with some irony to the time when as a student he gave an Emersonian address maintaining "The Main enterprise of the world . . . is the upbuilding of a man. The private life of one man shall be a more illustrious monarchy . . . than any kingdom in history." On the other hand he is disgusted by the slick contemporary pessimists who maintain that you must "sacrifice your poor, squawking, niggardly individuality which may be nothing anyway (from an analytic viewpoint) but a persistent infantile megalomania, or (from a Marxian point of view) a stinking little bourgeois property—to historical necessity." Against low sneering realists, Herzog prefers Romanticism. But on the other hand the objections to the cult of selfhood remain. Herzog oscillates continually and decides "perhaps a moratorium on definitions of human nature is now best." But secretly he really resists taking the view which degrades human worth, even though he knows what it is to long to escape from the burden of individuality. Secondly, the problem of freedom worries him: "people can be free now but the freedom doesn't have any content. It's like a howling emptiness." Technology has "created private life but gave nothing to fill it with." What does personal freedom mean; how much are we historically determined? Herzog thinks of Tolstoy's concept of freedom, and would seem to sympathise with it. *"That man is free whose condition is simple, truthful—real. To be free is to be released from historical limitation."* A dignified ideal—yet to step out into the street is to be buffeted by evidence of limitations.

Thirdly, Herzog refuses to believe the modern age is worse than any other and will not endorse pessimism. Spengler's notion of the decline of the West with its implication that the great age for Jews is gone forever, made him sick with rage as a youth: and when he reads that Heidegger talks about "the fall into the quotidian," he writes a letter to him asking *"When did this fall occur? Where were we standing when it happened?"* The potentialities of human life must be perennial. Though there is evil in the world he refuses to concentrate on it as the sole reality. He hears the most appalling evidence of sheer evil in the court room. The description of how a woman, without any tears or remorse, killed her child while her lover lay on the bed, watching and smoking, makes him feel violently sick. It is inexplicable, irremediable evil. "He opened his mouth to relieve the pressure he felt. He was wrung, and wrung again, and wrung again, again." It is this incident which makes him go to Chicago, intending to kill Madeleine and her lover because he has a notion they are mistreating his child. Of course, he has no murder in his heart and transcends his moment of aggressive impulse. His attitude to life is essentially creative not destructive. There is evil but he feels we must look away from it, beyond it. He feels that our age is too fond of regarding itself as monstrous, that an insidious prestige is now attached to "the negative." Vengefully, we deny all possibility of transcendence. The human imagination has been deflected and feeds on murder and death: *"Safe, comfortable people playing at crisis, alienation, apocalypse and desperation, make me sick,"* writes Herzog to a fellow professor. All this is the wrong path for civilisation. *"We love apoca-*

lypses too much, and crisis ethics, and florid extremism with its thrilling language. Excuse me, no. I've had all the monstrosity I want." To another he writes:

> *Has the filthy moment come when moral feeling dies, conscience disintegrates, and respect for liberty, law, public decency, all the rest collapse in cowardice, decadence, blood? . . . I can't accept this foolish dreariness. We are talking about the whole of mankind.*

He thinks that *"mankind is making it—making it in glory though deafened by the explosions of blood."* This is not callousness in Herzog; rather it is an insistence not only on the futility but on the dangers of dwelling on evil and death, nourishing the imagination on suffering and despair. Herzog wants to get away from the insidious attractions of nihilism. He is working for a change of heart.

These, then, are some of the ideas that possess Herzog. He is convinced of their importance; he wants to change the world. And Bellow is careful to show there is some comic presumption in all this along with a fair amount of egotism. Not for nothing is Herzog often caught looking at his own reflexion—he is unusually self-absorbed and self-important. Balance is restored by continual reminders of Herzog as a struggling physical creature; and he himself is continually mocking himself, undercutting his high mental intentions. We catch him at a transition point, waking to the ludicrous side of his conviction that "the progress of civilization—indeed, the survival of civilization—depended on the successes of Moses E. Herzog." He has it in him to want to be a new law-giver to mankind (as his name suggests) but his mind has reached a dangerous point when it can think "If I am right, the problem of the world's coherence, and all responsibility for it, becomes mine." Herzog himself comes to smile at himself, mentally legislating for the whole world while crammed into a subway car. After all, his own life is a "catalogue of errors"; he has been self-righteous, conceited in his suffering, monstrously egotistical, mediocre and merely "flirting a little with the transcendent." These are rigorous self criticisms; more usually it is the comic futility of his thinking that strikes him. At the same time his notions are precious and not invalidated. But for all his absurdity he is Herzog for good or bad. *"I am Herzog. I have to be that man. There is no one else to do it."* After smiling, he must return to his own Self and see the thing through." And properly to be that self he has to move beyond ideas, temporarily at least, and reestablish contact with ordinary reality.

This provides the ending of the book. Taking his daughter out, he has a car crash. He has some exhausting, troublesome hours with the police because of the revolver found on him. And this is where he really starts to relax, to descend "from his strange, spiraling flight of the last few days." He asks himself:

> Is this, by chance, the reality you have been looking for, Herzog, in your earnest Herzog way? Down in the ranks with other people—ordinary life? By yourself you can't determine which reality is real?

Bailed out by his brother he returns to his old country house. Taking an inventory of its great disorder and mess, he seems at the same time to be taking stock of the mess of his own life. He feels a strange joy, relaxed and liberated. Liberated, not only from Madeleine, but from excessive exhausting egotism, the curse of unending thought, the compulsive desire to explain everything and legislate mentally for the whole world. Madeleine said he was "sick with abstractions," and another woman tells him his "ideas get in the way." He feels there is some truth in this. He realises that perhaps he has been making an error in "going after reality with language."

A new calm starts to grow in him because he gradually ceases to strive for comprehension. "Go through what is comprehensible and you conclude that only the incomprehensible gives any light." He is sure that life is more than "mere facticity." Faith grows in him, as he starts to move beyond his verbalising, intellectualising, self-preoccupation and self-importance. Quoting approvingly the Whitman line—"Escaped from the life that exhibits itself"—he comes to a realisation of the dangers of that narcissism which makes an individual set himself up as a witness, an exemplar. He is learning a new humility, reacquainting himself with the ordinary with deep gladness. The curse is lifting and he is on the verge of a new health, stirred by "indefinite music within." Instead of worrying at the world with his theories he relaxes, "feeling that he was easily contained by everything about him." To calm his imagination, excited by a new happiness, he paints a piano for his daughter. At the same time "To God he jotted several lines":

> How my mind has struggled to make coherent sense. I have not been too good at it. But have desired to do your unknowable will, taking it and you, without symbols. Everything of intensest significance. Especially if divested of me.

He decides to "lay off certain persistent torments. To surrender the hyperactivity of this hyperactive face. But just to put it out instead to the radiance of the sun." He starts thinking about a more ordinary, sane future; instead of perverse self-communing—*"work. Real, relevant work."* "I mean to share with other human beings as far as possible and not destroy my remaining years in the same way. Herzog felt a deep, dizzy eagerness to *begin."* The prose of this last chapter is extremely specific and at the same time brimming with lyricism. It communicates Herzog's new delight in the simple objects in his house, and the loveliness of the summer garden; his dawning reverence for the concrete, the rich plenitude of the seen world. At the same time it catches his inner, trembling fervour as he moves beyond thought to a mood which is almost mystical. He is surcharged with a strange joy—mortal, but with transcendent intimations. *"This strange organization, I know it will die. And inside—something, something, happiness."*

The "spell" of the last few months is passing. "Perhaps he'd stop writing letters. Yes, that was what was coming, in fact. The knowledge that he was done with those letters." The last scene of the book leaves Herzog, stretched out on a couch, for the first time experiencing a true pervading quiet after the remorseless inner clamouring which has racked him throughout the book. "At this time he had no messages for anyone. Nothing. Not a single word." So the book ends. The resolution is completely internal. Externally there is still mess extending in all directions, but he has won through to a new attitude to it and seems at least able to reenter it in a more tranquil spirit. His new good intentions are not shown in action; we do not see the common life he intends to lead nor do we see him sharing his life with other human beings. The book takes Herzog to the end of his sickness and the promise of cure. The inward work has been done. He has endured thought and memory to the point of madness and breakdown: now he is passing beyond them into a mood of calm quiescent readiness. More genuinely than in any previous book by Bellow, we feel a novel, joyous sanity growing out of the neurotic exhaustion. No new meanings, no solutions: rather a change of heart, a turning to the sun. Not resignation but a profound "let be," accompanied by peace and a prayer of praise such as can only be uttered the other side of suffering.

Herzog: Freedom and Wit

Gabriel Josipovici

There's a lot of movement in Saul Bellow's *Herzog*, but the only action is a botched action: Herzog's failure to carry out his plan and kill his former wife Madeleine and her lover Valentine Gersbach. Anguished Herzog rushes from New York to the peace of Vineyard Haven and his friend Libbie but he's no sooner there than he decides to fly back to the capital. He spends the day in his apartment and the night with his current mistress; but the next day he's off again, to Chicago this time and his murderous mission. Instead of murder, however, he is involved in a minor traffic accident and hauled off to the police station for illegal possession of firearms. Bailed out by his brother, he ends up where we have first found him, in his vast decaying house in the middle of the Berkshires. It is not, however, all this flurry of meaningless activity that gives the book its sense of continuous turmoil. That comes from the ceaseless inner activity which grips Herzog and of which the external movement is merely a symptom. The greater part of the novel is taken up with Herzog by himself, writing compulsive letters to his friends, his enemies, the newspapers, politicians, "and at last to the dead, his own obscure dead and finally the famous dead." Sometimes the letters are only scribbled on odd bits of paper and promptly forgotten; most of the time they never get put onto paper at all. But though they seem to burst out of him wildly, spontaneously, and often peter out after no more than a sentence and nearly always before the end, a clear and consistent position does emerge from them, a position whose defining characteristic is that it cannot be reduced to any purely abstract statement, but which relates at almost every point to Herzog's own troubled life. To understand the novel we need to understand what this position is.

Like that of Swift in *A Tale of a Tub*, it can be expressed diagrammatically as the rejection of two false extremes. These Herzog calls "crisis ethics" and "potato love" respectively. Like Swift too, Herzog goes behind the labels that people and movements give themselves and brings out the essential similarity between many apparently disparate phenomena. And like Swift he believes that extremes meet and that crisis ethics and potato love are only facets of one attitude to both man and history. What meaning then do the terms have for him?

"Dear Doctor Professor Heidegger," writes Herzog, "I should like to know what you mean by the expression 'the fall into the quotidian.' When did this fall occur? Where were we standing when it happened?" The question is of course, rhetorical, but the ploy is the same as Swift's: by making concrete what his opponents keep at the level of metaphor he shocks us into an awareness of the implications of their position. He himself answers his questions later on, when he writes:

> Very tired of the modern form of historicism which sees in this civilization the defeat of the best hopes of Western religion and thought, what Heidegger calls the second Fall of Man into the quotidian or ordinary. No philosopher knows what the ordinary is, has not fallen into it deeply enough.

Nor is it simply German existentialism which is dominated by this idea. Herzog sees in it a Christian, and especially a Protestant view of history, one which regards "the present moment always as some crisis, some fall from classical greatness, some corruption or evil to be saved from." This idea has taken hold of modern man because it seems to be a way of saving him from himself and his daily responsibilities:

> Everybody was in the act. "History" gave everyone a free ride. The very Himmelsteins, who had never even read a book of metaphysics, were touting the Void as if it were so much salable real estate. This little demon was impregnated with modern ideas, and one in particular excited his terrible little heart: you must sacrifice your poor, squawking, niggardly individuality—which may be nothing anyway (from an analytic view point) but a persistent infantile megalomania, or (from a Marx-

ian point of view) a stinking little bourgeois property—to historical necessity. And to truth.

And what is truth? "Truth is true only as it brings down more disgrace and dreariness upon human beings, so that if it shows anything except evil it is illusion, and not truth." Facts are what's nasty, the rest is just idealism. The only way to get away from facts then is through ecstasy, through achieving an "inspired condition":

> This is thought to be attainable only in the negative and is so pursued in philosophy and literature as well as in sexual experience, or with the aid of narcotics, or in "philosophical," "gratuitous" crime and similar paths of horror. (It never seems to occur to such "criminals" that to behave with decency to another human being might also be "gratuitous.")

But all this, Herzog argues, all this talk of crisis and inspiration, is only a projection into history of private fantasies; they are ideas put out by intellectuals who long for the death of the intellect, something that will free them from the burden of daily living:

> Civilized individuals hate and resent the civilization that makes their lives possible. What they love is an imaginary human situation invented by their own genius and which they believe is the only true and the only human reality.

We must get it out of our heads that this is a doomed time; such talk is merely irresponsible, and is likely to lead to a loss of nerve which will bring about just such a doom:

> Are all the traditions used up, the beliefs done for, the consciousness of the masses not yet ready for the next development? Is this the full crisis of dissolution? Has the filthy moment come when moral feeling dies, conscience disintegrates, and respect for liberty, law, public decency, all the rest, collapses in cowardice, decadence, blood? Old Proudhon's visions of darkness and evil can't be passed over. But we mustn't forget how quickly the visions of genius become the canned goods of the intellectuals. The canned sauerkraut of Spengler's "Prussian Socialism," the commonplaces of the Wasteland outlook, the cheap mental stimulants of Alienation, the cant and rant of pipsqueaks about Inauthenticity and Forlornness. I can't accept this foolish dreariness. We are talking about the whole

life of mankind. The subject is too great, too deep for such weakness, cowardice. . . . A merely aesthetic critique of modern history! After the wars and mass killings!

It is time, argues Herzog, covering sheet after sheet with his desperate letters, it is time we stopped talking about human nature being this or that or the other thing. Total explanations are a delusion, the desire to see everything in terms of simple antitheses a sign of paranoia.

But is it possible to see life in any other way? Herzog discovers that the people who talk most about the "hard facts" of life are really the most sentimental, the believers in what he calls, talking of Eisenhower, "potato love": "The general won because he expressed low-grade universal potato love." But this too is a delusion, a form of self-pity, the wish to get rid of one's responsibilities by merging with the mass, the universal. Yet this merging is what Rousseau preached, and its appeal is enormous. Herzog is under no delusion about the power of words and ideas: "He took seriously Heinrich Heine's belief that the words of Rousseau had turned into the bloody machinery of Robespierre, that Kant and Fichte were deadlier than armies."

What is common to both the believers in crisis ethics and the believers in potato love is the notion that the world can be changed by a *fiat*, that if we will it hard enough we will find that our wishes and the reality of the world will coincide. It springs from the desperate need to shed the responsibility we are born with, a need which finds its ironic epigraph in what Tante Taube tells Herzog about making love with her first husband: "Kaplitzky-alehoshalom took care on everything. I didn't even looked." And yet the Romantics—for Herzog is in no doubt that if this is a Christian, and in particular a Protestant, movement, then it is with Romanticism that it gained its full momentum—the Romantics cannot so easily be refuted. For what model have we got to put in the place of the one they offer us? Herzog sympathises with T. E. Hulme's rejection of Romanticism, but he cannot agree with his solution of the problem:

> He wanted things to be clear, dry, spare, pure, cool, and hard. With this I think we can all sympathize. I too am repelled by the "dampness," as he called it, and the swarming of Romantic feelings. I see what a villain Rousseau was, and how degenerate. . . . But I do not see what we can answer when he says: "Je sens mon coeur et je connais les hommes." Bottled religion, on conservative principles—does that intend to deprive the heart of such powers—do you think? Hulme's follow-

ers made sterility their truth, confessing their impotence. This
was their passion.

The men Herzog admires are not the conservatives, who want to preserve
at all costs, for he sees that this too is a falsification of the reality of the
world in the interests of a private wish. No. It is men like Montaigne and
Pascal, politicians like Adlai Stevenson and Martin Luther King, who do
not shy away from the complexity and uniqueness of every situation by
opting for a single clear-cut solution, but on the contrary try to face and
understand and control, knowing that their work will take a long time,
that it will require patience above all things, and that it will constantly be
undermined by extremists. They accept man as he is, try to keep close to
the ins and outs of his thoughts and feelings. They accept a personal responsibility for history, a responsibility, notes Herzog, rooted in both Tes-
taments. And they are always beaten by the idealists.

It is by such idealists, all talking the same language of "truth" and
"hard facts," but all driven on only by the need to fulfil their private desires, that Herzog is surrounded. These people derive their power from
the fact that for them life is simple. They know the score. And they know
Herzog better than he knows himself. There is the psychiatrist, Dr. Edvig;
Sandor Himmelstein, the lawyer—"I know this isn't easy for you to hear,
but I better say it. Guys at our time of life must face facts. . . . I know
about suffering—we're on the same identical network." Above all, of
course, there are Madeleine, Herzog's former wife, and her lover Gersbach, his former friend. "She brought ideology into my life," Herzog recognises, at the end of the book. "Something to do with catastrophe." For
she and Gersbach never have enough of talking about Truth, though neither is very interested in the details of daily life. When Herzog, unable to
contain himself any longer, corrects Gersbach's dreadful Yiddish, the latter
brushes this aside and goes on with his man-to-man talk:

> "*Fe-be,* who cares. Maybe it's not so much your reputation as
> your egotism. You could be a real *mensch.* You've got it in you.
> But you're effing it up with all this egotistical shit. It's a big
> deal—such a valuable person dying for love. Grief. It's a lot of
> bull!"

And Herzog, looking at the man, with his game leg and fiery hair, is
forced to admit:

> Dealing with Valentine was like dealing with a king. He had a
> thick grip. . . . He *was* a king, an emotional king, and the

> depth of his heart was his kingdom. He appropriated all the
> emotions about him, as if by divine or spiritual right. . . . He
> was a big man, too big for anything but the truth.

What is important for Valentine Gersbach is the *intensity* of an experience,
not its content. This intensity, this physical glow which seems to guaran-
tee the genuineness of his emotion, goes into everything he does, whether
it's talking about Buber on television or advising Herzog about the nature
of life. And the same is true of Madeleine:

> Before Soloviev, she had talked of no one but Joseph de Mais-
> tre. And before de Maistre—Herzog made up the list—the
> French Revolution, Eleanor of Aquitaine, Schliemann's exca-
> vations at Troy, extrasensory perception, then tarot cards, then
> Christian Science, before that, Mirabeau; or was it mystery
> novels (Josephine Tey), or science fiction (Isaac Asimov)? The
> intensity was always high.

Excessive rationality, the inability to bear criticism, to accept ambiguity,
the desire to assert oneself continuously—all these are paranoic traits, Herzog is convinced, and all can be found in Madeleine. How can he leave his
children in the charge of people like her and Gersbach?

Yet are they unique? The whole of Western society seems to have ac-
quired these traits, and Herzog, in the course of his wild letters, finds their
roots in such things as the notion of outward composure in Calvinist soci-
eties, where each man, fearful of damnation, has to *behave* as one of the
elect in order to convince himself that he *is* one; in the fear of an increasingly mechanised world; in Rousseauistic notions of pity. There is no lack
of evidence for the historically minded. But it is also there in the present,
facing him, and Herzog doesn't know how to fight it. Even his current
mistress, Ramona, beautiful, exciting Ramona, whom Herzog likes so
much, is convinced that she understands Herzog's *real* needs better than he
does himself:

> To listen to Ramona, it was all very simple. She said she under-
> stood his needs better than he, and she might well be
> right. . . . She told Herzog that he was a better man than he
> knew—a deep man, beautiful (he could not help wincing when
> she said this), but sad, unable to take what his heart really de-
> sired, a man tempted by God, longing for grace, but escaping
> headlong from his salvation. . . . What he had to learn from
> her—while there was time; while he was still virile, his powers

substantially intact—was how to renew the spirit through the flesh (a precious vessel in which the spirit rested).

The difficulty with such arguments is that Herzog is perfectly well aware that they might all be true. Because he does not know what he *really* is, he cannot counter such assertions with any of his own, only with vague unease at such a formulation of the problem. Nor is it only Ramona who could be right. All of them—Madeleine, Gersbach, Edvig, Himmelstein— they might be right too, he might indeed be all that they say he is. Who is to say if they are wrong? Certainly not Herzog. And yet deep down inside him there remains the stubborn conviction that they *are* in some obscure way wrong, every one of them, including Ramona. The book, which charts his partial recovery from a mental breakdown, also shows his growing awareness of the nature of his own inarticulate attitudes and beliefs. He may not have the answers to the confident assertions of those who surround him, but that is perhaps a kind of strength, even if it makes him more vulnerable to their initial attacks. For one thing, he recognises very well the propensity within himself to fall for this kind of argument:

> It's about time I stopped laboring with this curse—I think, I
> figure things out. I see exactly what I should avoid. Then, all
> of a sudden, I'm in bed with that very thing, and making love
> to it. As with Madeleine. She seems to have filled a special
> need.

But even as he says this he knows he will labour under the curse all his life, that there will always be moments when he cries out under his breath, as he does earlier to Ramona: "Marry me! Be my wife! End my troubles!"—only to be immediately "staggered by his rashness, his weakness, and by the characteristic nature of such an outburst, for he saw how very neurotic and typical it was." Knowing this, though, he is determined not to be a victim, not to indulge in bitter self-criticism. He is what he is— why always be looking for a motive? His duty is to live. To be sane and to live and to look after his children.

His self-awareness does not stop with the recognition of his own general desire to give up, be safe, not have to make decisions. He realises too that just at this time he is in the grip of a particular violence, that these letters, this way of talking are not the actions of a normal man. And, recognising it, he can take steps to fight it, can even see that his own failure all along the line might not mean that his opponents are right but simply that he was confused and inadequate to the task. What he must avoid at

INTELLECTUAL AND EMOTIONAL ALIGNMENTS IN *HERZOG*

| Crisis Ethics | | Potato Love |
Dissolution of the self in universal TRUTH	Acceptance of responsibility for oneself	Dissolution of the self in universal LOVE
Calvin Kant Fichte Nietzsche Spengler Heidegger	Montaigne Pascal	Rousseau
Calvinism Marxism Freudianism Existentialism Russian mysticism (Soloviev, Berdyaev, etc.)		
Faust		
Black Muslims		Eisenhower
	Adlai Stevenson	
Tina Zokóly	Martin Luther King	
Madeleine Gersbach Dr Edvig Sandor Himmelstein Shapiro George Hoberly	Herzog Asphalter	Gersbach Sandor Himmelstein Mother Herzog Tante Taube

all costs is imposing his own pattern on reality, trying to get at the essence of people and slotting them into pigeon-holes in his mind. For man is always more complex than any of the models we create to explain him, be they Freudian, Jungian, Marxian, Thomist, or anything else. It may be, Herzog comes to see, that he cannot counter the image of himself that other people have, as being essentially this or that, simply because he has no essence, because he is not reducible in this way. The episode of Lucas Asphalter and his monkey is an essential element in this self-discovery. Asphalter, Herzog's old friend with whom he goes to stay when he returns to Chicago with the object of killing Gersbach, recounts how, after the death of his pet monkey, he felt he had no more to live for, and, on the advice of a psychoanalyst, tried to follow the prescriptions of the Hungarian analyst Tina Zokóly. These consist in such spiritual exercises as imagining your own death: you pretend you are already dead and try to conjure up the coffin and attendant paraphernalia. Asphalter, however, finds that with him this doesn't work. His mind keeps shifting from the scene of his death to the image of his enormously fat old aunt being carried down a ladder from one of the top windows of the building in which she lived when it caught fire, or to that of the whores who used to play baseball in the street outside the flophouse where they work. Asphalter recounts his failure to his friend in despair, but Herzog interrupts him excitedly:

> "Don't feel so bad, Luke. Now listen to me. Maybe I can tell you something about this. At least I can tell you how I see it. A man may say, 'From now on I'm going to speak the truth.' But the truth hears him and runs away and hides before he's even done speaking. There is something funny about the human condition, and civilised intelligence makes fun of its own ideas. This Tina Zokóly has got to be kidding, too."
>
> "I don't think so."
>
> "Then it's the old *memento mori*, the monk's skull on the table, brought up to date. And what good is that? It all goes back to those German existentialists who tell you how good dread is for you, how it saves you from distraction and gives you your freedom and makes you authentic. God is no more. But Death is. That's their story. And we live in a hedonistic world in which happiness is set up on a mechanical model. All you have to do is open your fly and grasp happiness. And so these other theorists introduce the tension of guilt and dread as a corrective. But human life is far subtler than any of its models, even these ingenious German models. Do we need to study *theories* of fear and anguish? This Tina Zokóly is a nonsensical woman. She tells you to practice overkill on yourself, and your intelligence answers her with wit."

Wit is the element that won't be captured, the individual response of a man trying hard to lose his individuality. It is grotesque, but reminds him that man is always something else, over and above any description of him that we can give. It is consciousness of this that leads Herzog at last to say (in his mind) to Madeleine and Gersbach: "Excuse me, therefore, sir and madam, but I reject your definitions of me."

But it is this too that stops Herzog from murdering Gersbach. As he looks through his own bathroom window and watches the man bathing his little daughter he is forced to realise that Gersbach is decent after all, perhaps even kind, according to his lights. Herzog, aware how much his condemnation of his former wife and her lover may be the result of his own uncontrollable emotions, understands in that brief moment that he could never kill. Especially not this man. Killing him is one more role into which he has tried to slip—a role and not himself. Leave the roles to the movies, creators of myths. He steps down from the window and goes his way. Something, however, must happen. All that pent-up emotion has to find an outlet. Typically, what happens is both farcical and banal, another victory of reality over any of its models. Herzog, taking out his little daughter for a drive the next day, is involved in an absurd car accident. No one is seriously hurt, but he is shaken by it, and especially by the confrontation at the police station with the furious Madeleine. How could he act like this, and show himself in this light to his daughter? Can she ever forgive him?

And yet the accident finally brings him down to earth "from his strange spiralling flight of the last few days." He can no longer run away from himself, he is, at last, up against the wall. Because, for all his talk of the ordinariness of life being the important thing and how one must be what one is and ask no questions, the whirlwind activity of those last few days did represent a flight from himself, from reality. Exactly like George Hoberly, Ramona's discarded lover, who tries to reawaken her sympathies by acts of deliberate self-destruction, Herzog has attempted to force from life an answer to the question: What am I? What am I really? The accident and its aftermath serves to free him from this compulsion. In a sense he bangs into reality. Not hard, but hard enough to remind him of what might have happened—like the blow the Green Knight delivers to Gawain, "nikking his neck." Herzog sees now how difficult it is to eradicate the notion of crisis from our minds, how we all unconsciously long for some one event that will change things irrevocably and tell us how from then on we are to lead our lives.

But now, back in his crumbling house in the heart of the countryside, he realises that "I have wanted to be cared for. I devoutly hoped Emerich would find me sick. But I have no intention of doing that—I am responsible, responsible to reason. . . . Responsible to the children." And, realising this, he finds a kind of peace:

Why must I be such a throb-hearted character? . . . But I am.
I am, and you can't teach old dogs. Myself is thus and so, and

will continue thus and so. And why fight it? My balance comes
from instability. Not organisation, or courage, as with other
people. It's tough, but that's how it is. On these terms I, too—
even I!—apprehend certain things. Perhaps the only way I'm
able to do it. Must play the instrument I've got.

Now at last he can answer Rousseau. True, the only kind of knowledge
we can have is what the heart feels, and yet "My face too blind, my mind
too limited, my instincts too narrow." We must not generalise from our
own heart, just learn to be content with it. And so, at the end, "I am
pretty well satisfied to be, to be just as it is willed, and for as long as I
may remain in occupancy."

Thus the letters come to an end. Herzog has no more messages for
anyone. And the novel too ends, leaving him there in his decaying mansion, waiting for Ramona—another mistake?—to arrive. The letters were
a symptom of his illness, but it is they which helped him through it. Like
Hamlet he deliberately exaggerated his condition, "as if by staggering he
could recover his balance . . . or by admitting a bit of madness could recover his senses." The others, Madeleine, Gersbach, Sandor Himmelstein,
George Hoberly, are the really sick ones, because they do not know they
are sick, imagine they are well: "It's possible to see that a man like Hoberly by falling apart intends to bear witness to the failure of individual existence. He proves it *can't work.*" Their madness lies in imagining that they
are sane, reasonable, *animal rationalis* instead of only *animal rationis capax.*
This is the other side to their insistence on Truth and their desperate desire
to label, define, organise, their inability to live with paradox or ambiguity—with wit. Herzog, recognising the infinite complexity of the human
psyche, will not judge someone like Madeleine's mother Tennie:

> Tennie took off her elaborate glasses, now making no effort to
> disguise her weeping. Her face, her nose reddened, and her
> eyes, shaped to make what seemed to Moses a crooked appeal,
> darkened blindly with tears. There was a measure of hypocrisy
> and calculation in Tennie's method, but behind this, again, was
> real feeling for her daughter and her husband; and behind this
> real feeling there was something still more meaningful and
> somber. Herzog was all too well aware of the layers upon lay-
> ers of reality—loathesomeness, arrogance, deceit, and then—
> God help us all—truth, as well.

Nor, in the end, will he judge Madeleine either. Judgement had best be
left to God. He's got enough to do making sense of his own life to try and

make sense of those of other people too. Because Herzog is so aware of the infinite regress of consciousness, he remains far saner than all the people who surround him, with their constant search for the one essential truth, the one revealing motive.

Yet if his weakness is his strength, his strength is also his weakness. If he is open to details, careful not to force the multitude of facts into a private mould, the very profusion of these facts, details, overwhelms him. He looks at everything as if he was seeing it for the first time, but the very sharpness of his perceptions is a sign of his instability: "A rat chewed into a package of bread, leaving the shape of its body in the layer of slices. Herzog ate the other half of the loaf spread with jam. He could share with rats too." The childhood memories, the physical details he notes in everything, all threaten to submerge him—"at first there was no pattern to the notes he made." It is all very well saying "foo" to all categories, but if one has responsibilities there is an urgent need to organise one's life. Herzog's follies and errors come as much from his unwillingness or inability to categorise as from his wish to force matters to a head. Reading Geraldine Portnoy's letter, in which she tells him how Gersbach is treating his children, he finds the handwriting keeps getting in the way of the meaning. He can see so many sides to every question that in the end he is inhibited from acting at all. He is aware that all reasoning is rationalised instinct, that Shapiro dribbling at the mouth as Madeleine serves up the food is as much a part of the picture as Shapiro's apocalyptic ideas. As Nietzsche saw, we can never sever the system from the man, we must always ask: "Why does *this* man advocate *this* system?" But it might be better for him to be a little less aware of such things. It is as though he is too close to the world to be able to make sense of it. Others are too far but he is too close.

This being so it is easy to see that the book, while charting his recovery from breakdown, simultaneously describes the final failure of his intellectual ambitions. It is clear by the end that Herzog will never write the sequel to his book on Romanticism and Christianity. The material is there, he's been lugging it around for years, but the will to put it together seems to be absent. No amount of letters is going to make up for that. Herzog knows—and it hurts him to acknowledge it—that to imagine he will write that book is to indulge in a Utopian dream.

But the reason for this failure is surely clear to us, if not to him. Were he to write the book he would himself be guilty of just the thing that he condemns in others: he would be setting up a model, albeit a highly sophisticated one, and saying: *this* is what man is like, this is what history *is*, this, ultimately, is what man is. As with the young Marcel and his literary ambitions, it is more than a failure of the will which keeps him from his task. It is the unconscious recognition that to give shape to the feelings of the heart is to falsify the experience, that intellectual history, no matter how subtle, must always leave out more than it puts in. No volume in the history of ideas can do justice to Herzog's insight into the infinite regress of human self-awareness. If, as soon as I say: "This is what I am," a part of me immediately dissociates itself from the definition, then what is required is a form that will convey the living person behind every speech and every gesture. What is required, in other words, is not history, but fiction, for only fiction can present the speaker as well as the words he speaks, can register the afterthought as well as the thought, and the afterthought to the afterthought, and the unspoken commentary on that. Thus Saul Bellow's *Herzog* emerges as the work which Herzog, the fictional hero of that book, found it impossible to write.

All Herzog is able to do is battle with his demons and let the future look after itself. But Bellow, through his fiction, has been able to articulate the variety and richness of the world without being overwhelmed by it and without on the other hand imposing upon it the rigid categorisation of the traditional novelist who only includes as much of the world as is necessary for his plot. Bellow has in fact succeeded in constructing a work which is an attack on the structuring activity of the mind; in conveying a sense of infinite mystery of human beings in a book which is a critique of the traditional link between motive and action; in keeping close to the twists and turns of a man's thoughts and feelings without either putting him in a straitjacket of theory or allowing the book to fall apart in chaos. He has done all this because his book is not called *Saul Bellow* but *Herzog*.

The name Moses Elkanah Herzog is to be found in James Joyce's own novel, *Ulysses*. By making use of it Bellow makes it clear from the start that he is writing fiction, not fact, much as Defoe, by using ordinary English names, tried to persuade his readers that he was writing fact and not fiction. But what is fact? Who am I? Who is Bellow? What is certain is that while writing *Herzog* he is Herzog and yet not Herzog, since he is always clear that he is the creator of Herzog. In his most recent novel Bellow writes ironically of Marx's vision of the proletarian revolution needing no historical models and comments on the colourful variety of present-day Americans: "They sought originality. They were obviously derivative. . . . Better . . . to accept the inevitability of imitation and then to imitate good things. The ancients had this right. Greatness without models? Inconceivable. One could not be the thing itself—Reality. One must be satisfied with the symbols." Thus, had he written directly about

himself, he would have fallen into the trap of either sentiment or proph-
ecy, have been either a Gersbach or a Shapiro. Writing fiction, he frees
himself from the dead weight of his own personality. "That suffering
hero" Herzog writes of himself, and, having written it, knows that he is
more than that since he has just formulated the description. And Bellow,
formulating the formulator, creates himself as he writes. Creates us too if
we follow Herzog and do not try to reduce the novel, as Madeleine and
the others tried to reduce him, to a single meaning, an essence. A piece of
fiction is like a man: to ask what it means and expect an answer is to destroy it. But, unlike a man, it has the power to stay alive forever. Or as
long, at least, as there are people to read it.

That Suffering Joker

Sarah Blacher Cohen

"Look at us, deafened, hampered, impeded, impaired and bowel-glutted with wise counsel and good precept, and the more plentiful our ideas the worse our headaches. So we ask, will some good creature pull out the plug and ease our disgusted hearts a little?" So Gooley MacDowell, Bellow's amateur Socrates and quirky monologist, addressing "the Hasbeens Club of Chicago," could very well be describing the plight of Moses Elkanah Herzog. Like Joseph, Leventhal, and Wilhelm, those lachrymose obstructed heroes of Bellow's victim literature, his vulnerable psyche is assailed with specious "wise counsel and good precept." His head is throbbing with painful recollections and warring insights. But like Augie and Henderson, those plucky challengers of Bellow's rebel literature, Herzog can "ease his disgusted heart" by calling into play his resilient sense of humor. He can eventually unload his weighty egotism and affirm the value of community. Herzog's affirmation, however, is not so effortlessly achieved. Whereas Augie and Henderson are part-time cogitators who only flirt with ideas, they can more readily break free of them to mingle with all kinds of people and extol their worth. Herzog, on the other hand, is the professional egghead whose ideas are his all-absorbing companions. He initially thinks he can understand and improve humanity through his sage speculations about it, even though he is removed from humanity. As it turns out, his mind becomes so "jammed with thoughts" and he grows so "sick with abstractions" that he is blinded to ordinary reality and the

From *Saul Bellow's Enigmatic Laughter*. © 1974 by Sarah Blacher Cohen. The University of Illinois Press, 1974.

existence of other human beings. Before he emerges from his cerebral re-treat, we witness the comedy of his tilting at intellectual windmills and being deterred from encountering the concrete texture of life. But we also observe the agony caused by his hyperactive introspection. "A prisoner of perception," he desperately wishes a reprieve from his sentence of hard mental labor to rejoin his fellow man. But just as no good creature pulls out Gooley's plug, no deus ex machina frees Herzog. He must struggle to extricate himself. The novel is a record of that struggle.

From Herzog's assessment of his experiences during the previous five days and from the memories of his recent and not-so-recent past precipi-tated by them, we learn how he has misconducted his life. Unlike his bib-lical namesake, he has spent his $20,000 patrimony, not on promised land, but on dilapidated property in the Massachusetts wilderness. He has strayed from the tribe of the Israelites to gain "a solid footing in white Anglo-Saxon Protestant America," yet he has not escaped from being the "Jew-man of Ludeyville." He has forsaken his orderly, benevolent first wife, only to have been forsaken by his disorderly, malevolent second wife. He has deteriorated from a productive, lucid scholar into a fallow, confused thinker. But because Herzog's misconduct is so extreme and ex-tends to all spheres of his life, it is difficult to take it altogether seriously. His woes are so innumerable and seemingly insoluble that his excessively dire circumstances make for a burlesque of the trials of Job.

Herzog is, however, more a self-ridiculing than a self-righteous Job. In the process of explaining, having it out, justifying, putting into perspec-tive, clarifying, and making amends, he is able to expose many of the comic flaws of his own character, including the diagnosis of his laughable chronic vanity. He recalls how as a youth he had been overly proud of his "soft handsome face, wasting [his] time in arrogant looks," and even now, in his faded middle age, he admits to being "vain of his muscles, the breadth and strength of his hands, the smoothness of his skin." But he can also cure himself of his infectious conceit with the most styptic humor of any of the Bellow heroes. Gazing admiringly at his reflection in the mir-ror, he hyperbolically compliments himself and then rationalizes away his self-love by hazarding an overly ingenious explanation for man's narcis-sism: "Oh, terrific—you look exquisite, Moses! Smashing! The primitive self-attachment of the human creature, so deep, so old it may have a cellu-lar origin." Bellow as omniscient narrator pulls down Herzog's vanity as well. In the courtroom scene he describes him as crossing his legs "with a certain style" and then impishly adds that "his elegance never deserted him even when he scratched himself." But it is Herzog's estimate of himself as an irresistible lady's man which is subject to the most devastating comic correction. Initially, he is confident he can pass for a "grand-looking man" and even in "fleeting moments" fancies himself "the young and glossy stud." But his self-mockery promptly undermines his inflated claims of extraordinary virility and disqualifies him from long-term participation in any kind of sexual olympics. Even though he succeeds in satisfying Ramona, "a true sack artist," he still jeeringly dubs himself the "petit-bourgeois Dionysian" or a "prince of the erotic Renaissance." And although he still has the "strength to carry a heavy-buttocked woman to the bed," he wryly concedes that "there were more faithful worshipers of Eros than Moses Elkanah Herzog."

Perhaps the best deflater of Herzog's affectation is the ever-present obtrusiveness of his body. Although he is not plagued by the "enormities and deformities" of a Henderson, or burdened by the "indecently big, spoiled" hulk of a Wilhelm, he is still embarrassed by the ravages of age upon his once delectable corpus and is thus comically *"tantalized"* by irksome physical imperatives. Herzog would, for example, like to resemble the handsome, beatific rabbi his mother had wanted him to become—but when he is dressed in bathing trunks and a straw hat, he observes with rueful humor how "gruesomely unlike a rabbi" he appears

> his face charged with heavy sadness, foolish utter longing of which a religious life might have purged him. That mouth!— heavy with desire and irreconcilable anger, the straight nose sometimes grim, the dark eyes! And his figure!—the long veins winding in his arms and filling in the hanging hands, an ancient system, of greater antiquity than the Jews themselves.

Even though he is outfitted in the latest summer resort fashions, he cannot accept himself as the dapper *bon vivant*, because he cannot avoid identifying himself with those "paunchy old men" with their "pitiful puckered knees and varicose veins, pelican bodies and . . . haggard faces under sporty caps." Most disappointing of all, Herzog cannot sustain the pose of the great humanitarian. Instead of improving the human condition, all he can do is take "a sleeping pill, to preserve himself." By perpetually calling attention to the corporeal side of Herzog, or by having Herzog himself wryly deprecate his body, Bellow not only makes his hero the target of laughter, but also batters away at his comic presumption.

Even if no mention were made of Herzog's uncomplimentary physical features, he would still be funny as the confirmed bungler or, as he describes himself, "the stumbling, ingenuous, burlap Moses." Like

Tommy Wilhelm, he is another *schlemiel*, that "agent of cultivated disability . . . [who] runs toward his goal over an obstacle course where he himself is responsible for strewing about most of the obstacles" (Chester E. Eisinger). Wilhelm allows vampires and confidence men to bleed him of his funds; in like manner Herzog's "dignified blundering" has financially exhausted him. He shamefacedly admits, "With me, money is not a medium. I am money's medium. It passes through me—taxes, insurance, mortgage, child support, rent, legal fees." Herzog is also derelict in his religious obligations, obligations which he usually takes seriously. Unlike Updike's Bech, the Jew as spawned by the Protestant imagination, who is familiar with only the ethnic clichés and sociological parodies of Judaism, Herzog is an authentic Jew who is deeply committed to the Jewish heritage. When he becomes too intimate with beloved infidels and is in danger of neglecting his own creed, he is especially severe with himself. Making love to his Oriental mistress, Sono, on her unclean, disheveled bed, he hyperbolically reproaches himself for being a renegade from the faith. "Have all the traditions, passions, renunciations, virtues, gems, and masterpieces of Hebrew discipline . . . brought me to these untidy green sheets and this rippled mattress?" In his courtship of Madeleine, when he commits the unpardonable sin of accompanying her to mass, he is appalled by the absurdity and sacrilege that he, a Jewish family man whose middle name, Elkanah, means "possessed by God," should be attending a service in the Catholic Church. Herzog amusingly but accurately characterizes his religious failings when he confesses to the God of the Old Testament, "Lord, I ran to fight in Thy holy cause, but kept tripping, never reached the scene of the struggle." Herzog is also a poor judge of women, especially when it comes to selecting a marriage partner. Just as Wilhelm "had made up his mind not to marry his wife, but ran off and got married," so Herzog knows what he "should avoid. Then, all of a sudden, [he's] in bed with that very thing, and making love to it." Instead of choosing the submissive, thrifty Sono, he marries the domineering, extravagant Madeleine. Herzog is, moreover, an unwitting accomplice to his own cuckoldry. While he obligingly spends four afternoons on the psychiatrist's couch, Valentine Gersbach conveniently spends his time in Madeleine's bed. Herzog even permits Gersbach to take Madeleine's diaphragm to her in Boston, where she had gone to save their marriage. Like Isaac Bashevis Singer's Gimpel the fool, who is repeatedly cuckolded yet continues to believe in his wife's innocence despite the most damning evidence of her adultery, Herzog believes Madeleine when she insists that Gersbach is not her lover but the "brother [she] never had." Later, of course, Herzog realizes the cruel joke that has been played on him, for which he himself has provided the climactic, humorous twist. Or, as he mordantly describes the *ménage à trois*, "I sometimes see all three of us as a comedy team . . . with me playing straight man." As a father, Herzog is also incompetent. Unlike the patriarchs of old who protected the entire tribe from injury and destruction, Herzog cannot even take his little daughter on an outing without almost killing her. Despite his fine intentions and his conscientious efforts, Herzog is still one of those "bungling child-men," "an incorrigible character, doing always the same stunts, repeating the same disgraces"— in other words, the *schlemiel*.

As a *schlemiel*, Herzog is chiefly responsible for his own "humiliating comedy of heartache." But like Wilhelm and Leventhal, Bellow's other obsessed abuse-seekers, he also relishes this heartache. As he says, "When a man's breast feels like a cage from which all the dark birds have flown— he is free, he is light. And he longs to have his vultures back again. He wants his customary struggles, his nameless, empty works, his anger, his afflictions and his sins." Unlike his tormented fictional brethren, however, Herzog recognizes the perverse delight he derives from anguish and can see the humor in such masochism. When he subjects himself to his own brutal self-scrutiny and finds himself grossly inadequate as a husband, father, son, brother, citizen, friend, lover, and thinker, he claims to be "satisfied with his own severity, positively enjoying the hardness and factual rigor of his judgment." Yet he undercuts the harshness of his self-criticism by wryly adding, "But how charming we remain, notwithstanding." Without benefit of a Tamkin or a Dahfu to clear his vision, he realizes that his entire life has been one prolonged love affair with suffering, what with "writhing under [Madeleine's] sharp elegant heel," lending "his attackers strength," and inflaming himself with "failure, denunciation, distortion." He is able to point up the inanity of such an existence by presenting a facetiously melodramatic account of its basic pattern. "I fall upon the thorns of life, I bleed. And what next? I get laid, I take a short holiday, but very soon after I fall upon those same thorns with gratification in pain, or suffering in joy—who knows what the mixture is."

Similarly, Herzog can see the humor in his chronic lamentation. This is not to say that he is without any genuine sorrows. He is not an Alexander Portnoy, whose chief rage is directed against a nasty Mommy and whose complaint is but a puerile temper tantrum interspersed with prurient exhibitionism. Herzog has experienced severe personal indignities and deserves a certain measure of commiseration. Yet, as Bellow has pointed out, "*Herzog* makes comic use of complaint." For example, when he considers telling Ramona his much rehearsed tale of victimization, he likens himself to "an addict struggling to kick the habit." Or recalling how he "suffered in style," he admits to turning his " 'personal life' into a circus, into gladiatorial combat." Fully recognizing his tendency toward hyperbolic confessions of woe, he, unlike the earlier Bellow protagonists, has the necessary detachment to call himself "that suffering joker."

While Herzog is amusing because he is a "real, genuine old Jewish type that digs the emotions" and compels others to "dig" his emotions, he is "to the point of death, 'comical' " because of the all-absorbing project he has undertaken, a project which throws him "out of gear with the fundamental norms and orders of human existence" (Nathan A. Scott, Jr., "The Bias of Comedy and the Narrow Escape into Faith"). Augie is obsessed with seeking a distinctive fate, and Henderson is driven to transcend human limitation; so Herzog has "tried to be a *marvelous* Herzog." As a high school youth, brought to a boil by Emerson, he fervently believes that "the main enterprise of the world . . . is the upbuilding of a man." As an adult he is still filled with "high cravings" for the good and the true. It is, according to Bellow, Herzog's obsession with being an exceptional individual that makes him so humorous: "I don't think that I've represented any really good men. . . . I often represent men who desire such qualities but seem unable to achieve them on any significant scale. . . . Herzog wants very much to have effective virtues. But that's a source of comedy in the book." Herzog does not wish to achieve merely personal excellence, to upbuild only himself. He is consumed with the far more lofty aim of making a significant intellectual contribution to society. He hopes to write a highly original, systematic study of the social ideas of the Romantics. It is his high-minded intention to come up with no less than a "new angle on the modern condition, showing how life could be lived by renewing universal connections; overturning the last of the Romantic errors about the uniqueness of the Self." While such a noble endeavor is most laudatory, it turns out to be most ludicrous, since it is such an inconceivably large order for even the best-equipped supplier of information. Bellow himself has commented on the "comic impossibility of arriving at a synthesis that can satisfy modern demands." In a *Chicago Tribune Books Today* interview he elaborates on this point with respect to *Herzog*:

> One of the sources of comedy in my book is the endless struggle of people to make sense of life and to sort out all the issues, and to get the proper historical perspective on oneself. . . . The whole world runs through your head like an oceanic tide and

you have to, for the sake of your balance and even your sanity, sort everything out. My hero makes use of a phrase coined by President Wilson's Vice President, who was a man named Marshall, a Hoosier cracker barrel philosopher, and a great wit, who said, "What this country needs is a good 5 cent cigar." Herzog translates this for himself as "What this country needs is a good 5 cent synthesis." We live in these tides of information and fact which sway us back and forth. . . . The human mind seems to be not prepared for this kind of unprecedented modern crisis, and it is the humor of that kind of floundering that I try to get into Herzog. Even the qualified intellectual doesn't know what he's doing.

Initially Herzog does not realize how absurd both he and his project are. He is supremely confident of his ability and feels that he can "wrap the subject up . . . pull the carpet from under all other scholars, show them what was what, stun them, expose their triviality once and for all." Yet he assures himself that he is motivated not by the need for personal acclaim, but by a sense of genuine responsibility to his fellow man. Indeed, he regards himself as "the man on whom the world depended for certain intellectual work, to change history, to influence the development of civilization." To accomplish such a momentous task, he deems it necessary to absent himself from society; only in splendid isolationism can he develop his splendid ideas. In a ramshackle hideaway he, like Thoreau, attempts to carry out "his plan for solitary self-sufficiency." His plan, however, soon goes awry. Instead of writing a work which takes "into account the revolutions and mass convulsions of the twentieth century," he becomes sidetracked by his own personal convulsions. Instead of elucidating Hegel's "ideas on consensus and civility," he suffers the deterioration of his own civility. Instead of defining "the importance of the 'law of the heart' in Western traditions," he is at a loss to define his own "throb-hearted" nature.

Unable to "legislate mentally" for mankind (Tony Tanner, *Saul Bellow*), let alone govern himself, Herzog heeds the promptings of his lawless id. Unable to cope with the more complicated issues of life, he copes with women. Yet Herzog is not consumed with achieving what Mailer in "The White Negro" describes as the "orgasm more apocalyptic than the one which preceded it." Since his need for order is ultimately stronger than his need for orgy, he can see the absurdity of his lust, revealing it to be "the most wretched form of human struggle, the very essence of slavery." Yet he cannot entirely free himself from this form of bondage. He ingeniously convinces himself that sexual gratification is essential to his health and well-being. He further rationalizes his personal need by generalizing it to a societal need. "The erotic," he authoritatively claims, "must be admitted to its rightful place, at last, in an emancipated society which understands the relation of sexual repression to sickness, war, property, money, totalitarianism." Bellow undoubtedly had such a remark in mind when he jocosely informed a French reviewer: "En Amérique, la sexualité est moins plaisir érotique qu'hygiène indispensable." Herzog devastates his own rationalization by suggesting a similar *reductio ad absurdum* conclusion that can be drawn from it: "Why, to get laid," he states with tongue in cheek, "is actually socially constructive and useful, an act of citizenship." Despite his mockery of the worth of sexual therapy, he is "powerless to reject the hedonistic joke of a mammoth industrial civilization," and he eagerly puts himself in the hands of Ramona, therapist par excellence. After a night-long treatment, he is still the same idiosyncratic Herzog with "his problems as unsolved as ever" in addition to "a lip made sore by biting and kissing."

Along with being the erotic playboy of the western world, Herzog is the erratic correspondent of the western world. Since his intellect is temporarily in a state of disrepair and thus incapable of providing his reading public with any sustained discussions of his views, he continually scribbles brief dispatches filled with his unfinished thoughts and private associations. Although he addresses these messages to political figures, psychiatrists, theologians, past and present philosophers, academic colleagues, living and dead relatives, and even to God, he never posts them. Joseph, unable to complete his essays on the Rationalists in an age of general irrationality, is driven to keep a journal to preserve his sanity; likewise Herzog, prevented from writing about the Romantics by his own tumultuous romances, must write his mental notes if he is to restore his balance—indeed, if he is to continue living. For, as he claims, he has always performed "elaborate abstract intellectual work . . . as if it were the struggle for survival," fully convinced that he "would die when thinking stopped." This is not the only reason for his letter-writing. It also enables him to put "his troubles into high-minded categories," allowing him to be dispassionate and even profound, meanwhile disguising the fact that he is settling his personal grievances. Through these letters he also plays the game of one-upmanship with the masterminds of all time. Since he has not been able to write a work which confounded and dazzled everyone, he is compelled to expose loopholes in the experts' thinking, furnish brilliant corrections, and overwhelm them with his own flawless theories. But Herzog soon realizes how inane it is for him to match wits with disembodied spirits, no matter how much his battered ego requires a victory. Even more disconcerting is his discovery that in these letters he has tried to impose his ideas on others. Therefore he, too, like the Reality Instructors he detests, is "a very special sort of lunatic [who] expects to inculcate his principles." Yet this was not his conscious intention. What he had essentially wished to do through his "helter-skelter" correspondence "in all directions" was to fathom the complexities of history and society in order to make sense of his own complexities. Also, by engaging in imaginary communication with people in the here and the hereafter, he had hoped to break out of his solitary confinement. But he ends up erecting verbal structures which only further distort the view of the world he is trying to understand and further separate him from the people he is trying to reach.

Love-making and letter-writing are not Herzog's only diversions when his "all-powerful human intellect . . . has no real occupation." He also plays the role of the mad avenger. When he learns that his arch-rival, Valentine Gersbach, has locked his little daughter in a car at night to prevent her from hearing his argument with Madeleine, Herzog is outraged. He clamors for justice. He fantasies how he will annihilate the guilty pair. But for the time being he is not prompted to act out this fantasy. Only after he encounters the brutality of actual child-killers in a New York courtroom is he driven to seek revenge upon Madeleine and Valentine.

Just as Henderson's confrontation with the malignant lion who kills Dahfu forces him to recognize his own evasions of evil and death, Herzog's hearing of the crimes of others leads him to acknowledge his own crimes. Initially, however, as he waits for his lawyer in the hall of justice, he regards himself as the thoroughly upright professor, the "Jesus" who has no "flies" on him. But after witnessing one case of human depravity after another, his composure is visibly shaken. Unlike Leventhal, he does not attribute his uneasiness to the presence of evil in an Allbee; unlike Joseph, he cannot be entirely convinced that only the next man is "full of instinctive bloody rages, licentious and unruly from his earliest days, an animal who had to be tamed." Rather, Herzog has the "floating suspicion" that he, too, has his own generous endowment of evil. He begins to realize that his ridiculous obsession to become "a marvelous Herzog" has not purged him of his wickedness, but has merely forced it to go into hiding. On the surface, therefore, he appears to be the tamed animal, the "pet goose" who, like the outwardly submissive Tommy Wilhelm, makes the "psychic offer—meekness in exchange for preferential treatment." If any evil were to be committed, he would never be the perpetrator of it.

"Others were appointed to do it to him, and then to be accused (by him) of wickedness." But for the most part, striving for perfection and pursuing his humane studies in the "coop of his privacy," he had been shielded from the vile side of life. Even as a teenager he had tried to escape the most unpleasant reality of all—death. Henderson fled to Africa, "the real past," to avoid death; so Herzog, "a bookish, callow boy," immersed himself in Spengler's Magian era to ignore the fact that his mother was dying. He was incensed that as a Jew he was considered a relic, but he did not seem particularly distressed that his mother, already a walking skeleton, was soon to be a corpse. When her eyes finally told him, "My son, this is death," Herzog reflects: "I chose not to read this text." As the insulated young intellectual, he would rather read "*The Decline of the West,* preferring to consider cultural decline than personal decline" (John J. Clayton). But in the courtroom Herzog cannot fail to recognize personal decline, nor can his scholar's immunity to evil prevail. He can no longer be comforted by the naive view that "once cruelty has been described in books it is ended." When he comes up against real cruelty—the abysmal neglect and then fiendish murder of an innocent child—he experiences in full force "the monstrousness of life." Identifying his own daughter with the slain child, and Madeleine and Valentine with the villainous mother and her lover, he can no longer suppress his own internal evil—the "acrid fluid in his mouth that had to be swallowed." Moses, the would-be lawgiver, therefore flies to Chicago to violate the most sacred commandment, "Thou shalt not kill." But like Bellow's other outraged heroes, with the possible exception of Henderson, he only murders in his imagination. Far from being a Stephen Rojack, the college professor who in Mailer's *An American Dream* actually does kill his wife, Herzog only poses as the fierce vindicator, never firing his father's antique pistol. When he sees Madeleine and Valentine, he is able to dissociate them from the heinous criminals he had recently witnessed. And when he catches sight of his little daughter, not beaten to death but very much alive and thoroughly enjoying her bath, he does not have to commit a Valentine massacre. He immediately recognizes the absurdity of the revenge which has consumed him. As Bellow indicates, Herzog's "intended violence turned into *theater,* into something ludicrous. He was not ready to make such a complete fool of himself."

Herzog's foolishness, however, is not at an end. When he finally gets to spend the afternoon with his daughter, he has an automobile accident. The accident is not his fault, but concealing his father's "clumsy horse pistol with [its] two cartridges" is his fault and is considered a misdemeanor by the police. Too late, he realizes that he should have left the revolver in his friend's apartment and "stopped being quixotic." Booked for carrying a loaded weapon, he and his daughter are taken to the police station. Although this is what he may have been seeking in his "earnest Herzog way"—to be "down in the ranks with other people, ordinary life"—he has to admit that this was an inane way of going about it. He had to smash a car, fracture his ribs, and terrify his little girl to "determine which reality is real." As he sardonically remarks, "You burn the house to roast the pig. It was the way humankind always roasted pigs." But Herzog is now through burning houses. In his jail cell he vows to bring down the curtain on his "daily comedy." "No more of this hectic, heart-rent, theatrical window-peering; no more collision, fainting, you-fight-'im-'e-cry encounters, confrontations." When Herzog is freed from his brief imprisonment, he is also freed of most of his comic vices.

Returning to his Berkshire haven, Herzog is able to divest himself of his former affectation—in the words of Whitman, to escape "from the life that exhibits itself." He can surrender his sorrows without feeling robbed of them; he can give up his sackcloth and ashes without feeling naked. Unlike Tommy Wilhelm, he is now able to go "with joy" and not think he is committing "adultery." As he greets the radiance of the sun, he is filled with "true cheerfulness, not the seeming sanguinity of the Epicureans, nor the strategic buoyancy of the heartbroken."

Herzog has also ceased being a "junkie—on thought." He has given up what Bellow describes in *The Last Analysis* as "the mind's comical struggle for survival in an environment of Ideas." When Herzog now encounters a myriad of facts, he is not compelled to explain their precise meaning or to organize them in any systematic way. When he finds a note card in his study reminding him "to do justice to Condorcet," he does not have to exhaust himself championing any theorist who agrees with him or lash out at any other who opposes him. No longer placing such a high premium on intellectuality for its own sake, Herzog comes to understand [in Bellow's words] that "habit, custom, tendency, temperament, inheritance and the power to recognize real and human facts have equal weight with ideas." This does not mean that Herzog will never return to his intellectual endeavors, yet we are assured that he will not rely exclusively on solitary intellection and thereby lose his grasp on ordinary reality. He has already discovered what distortions and strange views such separatism produces. Recognizing that he can achieve meaning not in isolation, but in the midst of other men, Herzog vows, "I mean to share with other human beings as far as possible and not destroy my remaining years in the same way."

Above all, Herzog is no longer one of those intellectuals who love only "an imaginary human situation invented by their own genius." Like Henderson after his lion shock therapy, he can accept reality for what it is without altering it to suit his fancy. As Herzog inspects his property, he can accept both the incomparable beauty of the land and the ugly ruins beyond repair, the contaminated well water and the overgrown garden—"hopeless—past regretting." He can accept his tumbledown house, knowing full well that he will never have the strength to renovate it. He is no longer disgusted with the "ruins of his scholarly enterprise," nor is he outraged or envious that his sanctuary has become the trysting place for village lovers. Although saddened by the skeletons of young birds trapped in the drained toilet bowl, he can even accept their untimely death. Perhaps more significant, he is able to accept the eventuality of his own death, not with rancor but with a "holy feeling." With the same "spirit of comedy" with which his mother had tried to prove to him that Adam was created out of dust, and with the same "wit you can have only when you consider death very plainly," Herzog declares, "I look at myself and see chest, thighs, feet—a head. This strange organization, I know it will die." Meanwhile, even though his face is "too blind," his "mind too limited," and his "instincts too narrow," he opts to make do with his flawed being during his brief span of survival. Herzog ends up being "the comic man" whom Nathan Scott defines as the "contingent, imperfect, earth-bound creature" whose function it is "to awaken in us a lively recognition of what in fact our true status is." Herzog, as comic man,

> asks us not to be afraid to acknowledge that we are only human and that our residence is not in the heavens. And he asks us to examine critically all the spurious stratagems that we employ to evade a frank acceptance of our finitude, whether they be those of bourgeois worldliness or of philosophical and religious mysticism. What the comic man cannot abide is the man who will not consent to be simply a man, who cannot tolerate the thought of himself as an incomplete and conditioned creature of a particular time and a particular space.

In addition to viewing himself as comic man, Herzog is endowed with "passionate satire" which enables him to express what is worthy of laughter in the next fellow. Because he has been "swindled, conned [and] manipulated" by chance acquaintances and supposed friends alike, his satire is, for the most part, of the harsh Juvenalian brand. Unlike Augie, whose resilient youth and larky good nature allow him to playfully mock and genially exonerate his exploiters, Herzog is initially too embittered to contain his vitriol or even to dilute it. All he can do is transform it into corrosive wit and wait for the opportunity to discharge it. But since Herzog has limited his contact with most people, they exist only as fleeting figures in his thoughts. He therefore cannot furnish any sustained caustic analysis of what makes them funny; he can merely fulminate about their most salient comic features. Aunt Zelda he scathingly dismisses as the vain and hypocritical suburban *hausfrau* who fancies herself a cut above the other ladies of the neighborhood, even though she, too, dyes her hair, wears "purplish lines on her lids," and believes that every married girl is entitled to "nightly erotic gratification" along with every conceivable luxury. Dr. Edvig, the Protestant Freudian, he lampoons as the unprofessional psychiatrist who prefers to treat Madeleine rather than Herzog, since she has a more intriguing body and a leaning toward Christianity. Shapiro, the intellectual historian, he denounces both as a ridiculously affected academician and as the gluttonous offspring of a rotten apple vendor. The lawyers Himmelstein and Simkin he ambivalently views as representative mass men foully "cutting everybody down to size" and as a pair of old-fashioned Jews, oozing with "schmaltzy" affection.

It is only when Herzog recalls the droll characters who inhabited his childhood that he employs the milder Horatian kind of satire. Since his nostalgia rather than his wrath has been kindled, he is prompted to take a wistful inventory of all the odd dwellers of Napoleon Street. Although he detects their flaws and itemizes them with benign laughter, he still wants to retain these imperfect creatures as permanent fixtures in his memory. An unexpected meeting with Nachman, a former grade school friend, causes Herzog to begin his own ruefully humorous remembrance of things past. He calls to mind Nachman's father, the tyrannical, Mongolian-hued Hebrew teacher who immediately assumed that all of his pupils were not only bastards and thieves but, far worse, devourers of ham and bacon. Far less threatening was Nachman's uncle, Ravitch, the incurable tipster, who, having lost his wife and children in the Russian Revolution, boarded with the Herzogs. Nightly serenading the family with alternate snatches from Hebrew liturgy and popular tunes, this ineffectual Jewish drunkard, unable to become cheerful even when inebriated, evoked both laughter and tears. A greater disturber of the peace was Aunt Zipporah, who, like Augie March's Grandma Lausch, was "witty, grudging, at war with everyone." A sharp-tongued critic of the Herzog pursuit of "dignities, honors," she strove only for material objects. Father Herzog, just the opposite of his crass sister, was the refined though improvident gentleman. Although he "could calculate percentages mentally at high speed," he was slow to realize any of the profits. Having repeatedly failed as a businessman, he still prided himself on being a fierce struggler. Herzog amusingly remembers that, as with himself, all of "Papa's violence went into the drama of his life, into family strife, and sentiment."

There are characters whom Herzog wants to blot out of his memory—the two who have most sorely wronged him, Valentine and Madeleine. Yet his hatred of them keeps them uppermost in his mind. Unlike the Napoleon Street figures whose defects become less offensive and even endearing through his mental revival of them, the aberrations of the two "love actors" are magnified through Herzog's compulsive dwelling upon them. They alone incur his most searing and unrelenting invective.

Valentine, "a paper imitation of the real man of heart" (David D. Galloway, "Moses-Bloom-Herzog: Bellow's Everyman"), has many of the same comic vices as Herzog, only his vices are more extreme. Valentine also evokes more unsympathetic laughter than Herzog, since he does not have his redeeming virtue of self-mockery. Although Valentine has a more advanced case of ridiculous vanity than Herzog—jauntily wearing the flashy apparel which Herzog is ashamed to purchase and fancying himself the prize cock of the walk—never once does he wryly puncture his full-blown conceit.

Valentine considers himself the prize sufferer as well. Herzog's psychic scars are obviously insignificant compared to his devastating physical wound—the amputation of his leg at the age of seven. Unlike Herzog, who makes fun of his own feeble bids for sympathy, Valentine without the slightest trace of levity demands as just compensation all the compassion the world can give him. "A frequent weeper of distinguished emotional power," he generally obtains the desired response. But a good part of the time he ends up receiving the greatest share of compassion from himself. Valentine has a monopoly on other kinds of emotion also. As Herzog sardonically says of him, "He *was* a king, an emotional king, and the depth of his heart was his kingdom." However, once any serious emotions become Valentine's possessions, they soon sound like foolish dime-store sentiments.

Valentine is also the caricature of the "real, genuine old Jewish type." Vastly ignorant of the religious, ethical, and cultural traditions of Judaism, he thinks he can pass himself off as the choicest of the chosen people by writing heart-rending poems about his quaint old Jewish grandfather and delivering easily understood lectures on Martin Buber to Hadassah groups. Above all, he purposely loads his speech with vivid Yiddish expressions.

Herzog jeeringly informs us that Valentine grossly misuses and mispro-
nounces most of these; thus he is an *ersatz* Jew as well as an *ersatz* man of
feeling.

Valentine is most ludicrous in his specious pose as the intellectual.
Whereas Herzog experiences great difficulty in making sense out of very
complex ideas, Valentine, the great "popularizer," has no trouble in sim-
plifying such ideas so that they are readily understood by the average
third-grade viewer of television. Whereas Herzog fails to produce a grand
synthesis of all existing knowledge, Valentine is "a regular Goethe [who]
finished all your sentences, rephrased all your thoughts, explained everything." Whereas Herzog actively engages in honest battle with the great
minds of past and present, Valentine, the television "ringmaster," pits one
contemporary thinker against another and passively looks on as they feign
tearing into each other. Whereas Herzog desperately wishes to leave his
ivory tower to share his talents with other human beings, Valentine, readily established in the world at large, effortlessly gives of himself and is able
to be all things to all people. "With pinochle players he plays pinochle,
with rabbis it's Martin Buber, with the Hyde Park Madrigal society he
sings Madrigals." Whereas Herzog gives thoughtful advice to his disturbed friend Lucas Asphalter, the "lectures Gersbach read [Herzog]
. . . were . . . a parody of the intellectual's desire for higher meaning,
depth, quality." Valentine Gersbach is a superb example of the buffoon as
thinker, "the kind of man who makes intellectuals wish they were dead
when they hear him parroting their words" (Irving Howe, "Odysseus,
Flat on His Back").

In George Meredith's opinion, the higher the comedy, the more
prominent the part women play in it ("An Essay on Comedy"). While this
is not the case in most of Bellow's novels, where the female characters
have no significant effect upon their menfolk, it is the case in *Herzog*,
where Madeleine plays a leading role in the hero's "painful emotional
comed[y]." The Madeleine we see, however, is not a fully realized personality, but the grotesquely funny creature that emerges from Herzog's angry recollections and perverse fantasies. Lacking any fixed psychic
identity, she is above all the quirky dilettante, much like Henderson's
wives who, in the earlier versions of that novel, are by turns intensely interested in the Crimean War, Kierkegaard, Jung, and leprosy. The only
difference is that Madeleine's tastes are more diversified and that she pursues each of them with a vengeance, albeit a short-lived one. Like the
predators of Bellow's other novels, the imposters Allbee and Tamkin, she
exhibits manifestations of in-authenticity—a flare for theatrics and an ob-

session with role-playing. When Herzog first meets her, she is in fact caught up with acting the Catholic convert. Not only does she relish transforming herself into "a woman of forty—some white, hysterical, genuflecting hypochondriac of the church aisles"; she especially looks forward to confessing her sins to the eminent Monsignor Hilton, the proselyter of celebrities. But after she falls prey to the lascivious Jew, she feels too sullied to take communion and thus deprives herself of an invaluable association with one of the most famous Princes of the Church. Madeleine, then, leaves off being the "high-minded Christian lady" to become the "queen of the intellectuals." She is amusingly unconvincing as a practicing Catholic; she is also unbelievable as a genuine bluestocking. This is not to suggest that she is without any intellectual passions. She has, to be sure, been consumed with Soloviev, Joseph de Maistre, "the French Revolution, Eleanor of Aquitaine, Schliemann's excavations at Troy, extrasensory perception . . . then Christian Science, before that, Mirabeau." But Herzog informs us that her overriding interest is in reading murder mysteries and gossip columns. When she isn't straining her eyes over the printed word, she is out making costly purchases at the most elegant shops. Yet, absurdly enough, she has illusions of invading and taking possession of Herzog's intellectual stamping grounds, when in fact her constantly shifting enthusiasms would indicate that she is incapable of even self-possession.

Along with fancying herself the bluestocking *extraordinaire*, Madeleine considers herself the grand lady. With her affected British accent, "[her] patrician style" and "the crazy clear hauteur of [her] eyes," she tries to conceal her unrefined bohemian background. But frequently her crude self humorously bursts out of hiding. That she never bothers to clean up the eggshells, chop bones [and] tin cans under the table, under the sofa" is not in itself a sign of poor breeding, since noblewomen were never meant to be ignoble servants. But her tongue-lashing, fouler than any fishwife's, and her physical attacks, more vicious than any street fighter's, indicate that she is not the lofty individual she represents herself to be. Despite the fact that we are limited to Herzog's impression of Madeleine, we have to concede that his general assessment of her is not only clever but to some degree accurate: "Ah, this Madeleine is a strange person, to be so proud but not well wiped . . . —such a mixed mind of pure diamond and Woolworth glass."

If Madeleine is the bizarrely comic *belle dame sans merci,* then Ramona Donselle is the comically pathetic woman with too much *merci.* Not only does she give Herzog "room . . . in her soul, and . . . the embrace of her body"; she also supplies him with "asylum, shrimp, wine, music, flowers, sympathy." And if for some reason he could not sexually satisfy her, she would understand. "If anything, such humiliations would challenge or intrigue her, bring out her generosity."

In addition to being the excessively understanding woman, Ramona strains to be the *femme fatale*. But since she is approaching the desperate age of thirty-eight, her performances as a "tough Spanish broad" or one of those tarts in a "girlie magazine" turn out to be more silly than seductive. Although Herzog ultimately succumbs to her contrived charms, he sees that beneath her masquerade she is the fatigued middle-aged woman who very much wants a husband. If she must perform elaborate rituals to secure one, she is willing to do so. Thus Ramona's "erotic monkey-shines" prove more pathetic than amusing.

Ramona is totally amusing as theoretician of sex and sensibility. Trusting in the power of positive love-making, she urges Herzog to give full expression to his instincts and revel in her style of hedonism. It is her firm conviction that sexual release can eliminate man's "constitutional tension of whatever origin," along with curing the world of most of its ills. Should one fail to satisfy the needs of the body, she is certain it would be a "surrender to malignancy, capitulating to the death instinct." To lend support to her claim, Ramona not only quotes "Catullus and the great love poets of all times," but also cites the unimpeachable conclusions of such neo-Freudians as Marcuse and N. O. Brown. Despite her "florid" lecturing and her exuberant practical demonstrations, she is unable to convince Herzog that "the body is a spiritual fact, the instrument of the soul." Like the passive resister Augie March, Herzog finds such theorizing, even Ramona's ridiculous brand of it, a "dangerous temptation [which] can only lead to more high-minded mistakes." By making Ramona out to be the caricatured sensualist, Bellow discredits the belief in that kind of indulgence which does not allow for any self-regulating principles.

While Herzog focuses his comic lens primarily on his own flaws and the flaws of those close to him, he occasionally directs it outward at mankind in general. Although he sometimes transforms his personal spite into public scorn, the incisiveness of his insights cannot be denied. They are not "sophomoric tag-lines," as Poirier claims, but expressions of a gifted intelligence which enlarge a tale of private folly into a wide-ranging ideological comedy. Unlike Joseph, whose social indictment is but an inchoate quarrel with the profiteering, war-mongering usurpers of his freedom, or Augie and Henderson, who never stop moving long enough to make any sustained inquiries as to what bothers them in the external world, Herzog is the painstaking examiner of many of the mid-twentieth century's inane practices and values. Yet his unsent letters, the vehicles for his criticism, are not, like Norman Mailer's *Presidential Letters*, exclusively of the editorial axe-grinding variety; nor do they reek of the author's sense of himself as intellectual saviour of mankind. They are instead expressions of a man who, because he occasionally emerges from Plato's cave and has unimpaired glimpses of reality, is in a position to expose the faulty vision of those who are still in the cave and can see only the shadow of things. He does not presume that his exposure will cause humanity to vacate entirely from the realm of appearances. He would be satisfied if his perception of the disparity between the actual and the fancied would every now and then shatter illusions and promote lucidity.

Chaotically and arbitrarily dispersed throughout the narrative, Herzog's letters vary in length and concerns. Their degree of seriousness depends upon the importance he ascribes to the subjects he is discussing. When, for example, he happens to think about the American style of bureaucracy, he complains of the Internal Revenue regulations which "turn us into a nation of bookkeepers" so that "the life of every citizen is becoming a business." Since man's pursestrings rather than his heartstrings are most at issue, Herzog's pique is playfully expressed. But when he considers the country's insane nuclear policies which could endanger the lives of his own children and the entire population, he becomes one of those "bitter Voltairean types whose souls are filled with angry satire and who keep looking for the keenest, most poisonous word." In a letter to the *New York Times* he directs his angry satire at Dr. Teller, whose remark about tight pants affecting the gonads more than fallout is grossly misleading, and at Dr. Strawforth, whose "Philosophy of Risk," the specious comparison of "human life to Risk Capital in business," could trigger rather than deter a nuclear holocaust. Herzog mordantly observes that we prudent citizens are not innocent victims, for we willingly entrust our safety to such careless annihilation experts and persist in the belief that the "universe was made for our safe use." Because Herzog has harbored a similar delusion in his private life, he is compelled to ridicule it by presenting a ludicrous example of such thinking. "Light travels at a quarter of a million miles per second so that we can see to comb our hair or to read in the paper that ham hocks are cheaper than yesterday." Meanwhile, protected by such childish, erroneous notions, we remain at the mercy of those who have the power to obliterate us. And so Herzog ruefully concludes that de Tocqueville's impression of the American democratic society was incorrect, since its strongest impulse is not toward well-being, but toward self-destruction.

Herzog also takes the American democratic society to task for its lack of political acumen. Since he never does enter "politics in the Aristotelian sense," he does the next best thing: he becomes the scathing assessor of national affairs. Although his assessment does not resemble the homely debunking of a Will Rogers and would never induce people to acknowledge what foolish political mortals they are, it does in its own urbane, sophisticated fashion reveal the fatuities of the Eisenhower era and sardonically censures the silent generation responsible for them. In a letter to Governor Stevenson, Herzog, the vocal majority of one, bitterly notes that instead of allowing intelligence to work for the public good, the people reject "mentality and its images, ideas, perhaps mistrusting them as foreign." Instead of basing their choice of a president on sound judgment, they permit themselves to be swayed by degenerate sentimental affection, or what Herzog mockingly terms "low-grade universal potato love." They bypass the intense humanist, Adlai, and pick as their standard-bearer the low-keyed military hero, Ike. They do not object to his appointing corporation lawyers and executives, those whom Herzog with tongue in cheek calls "Industrial Statesmen," to determine what America's aims should be. The people unquestioningly accept the Statesmen's "collection of loyal, helpful statements to inspire us in the struggle against the Communist enemy" and devote their energies to manufacturing commodities in no way germane to their needs. Overly deferential to authority, the majority are content to be not Pascal's "thinking reeds," but "reed[s] bending before centrally generated winds." Given such a state of affairs, Herzog can only mordantly conclude, "So things go on as before with those who think a great deal and effect nothing, and those who think nothing evidently doing it all."

The Church, too, is subject to Herzog's wry scrutiny. His scrutiny, however, is colored by personal bias. Because Monsignor Hilton had been his rival for Madeleine's affections, and had been revered by her as the fount of all knowledge, Herzog transfers his animus for the man onto the institution he represents. Not only does he label the Church's claim of "universal understanding" to be a "harmful, Prussian delusion," but he also punctures this delusion by stating, "Readiness to answer all questions is the infallible sign of stupidity." Herzog's other objection to the Church has nothing to do with the waging of private vendettas. Angered by the maltreatment of others for a change, he chastens the clergy for its scant regard for the impoverished masses. While they purport to aid the indigent, they have done nothing constructive to eliminate the ugly poverty existing everywhere. If they genuinely tried to persuade the affluent to share their wealth, they would alienate their principal benefactors and be deprived of their own creaturely comforts. Out of self-interest, then, they minister only to the spiritual needs of their charges. And so the beggars still exist, whose wretchedness continues to make the rich men feel all the more superior because of their riches. As Herzog ironically observes, "Skid Row is the contrasting institution, therefore necessary. . . . Because of Lazarus, Dives gets an extra kick, a bonus, from his luxuries." But Herzog's severest indictment is leveled at Dr. Edvig's Protestant Freudian version of Christianity for its depreciation of mankind. Like Augie March, who inveighs against the prevailing low estimate of man, Herzog cannot abide Calvin's "lousy, cringing, grudging conception of human nature." Buttressed by the Jewish faith in the blessedness of creation and the sanctity of the temporal, Herzog ridicules that "Christian view of history" which sees "the present moment always as some crisis, some fall from classical greatness, some corruption of evil to be saved from."

Even greater peddlars of doom are those pseudo-intellectual secular pessimists who have appropriated "visions of genius" and in the process have perverted their meaning. In many of his essays and lectures Bellow has tried through wit and wily argument to upset their rotten pushcarts and run them out of business. In his earlier novels his heroes also made sporadic attempts to ferret them out and give them their eviction notices. But it is Herzog who most relentlessly pursues them, devastates them with his gall, and drives them into bankruptcy. He first exposes them as "pipsqueaks" ranting "about Inauthenticity and Forlornness" and then denigrates the secondhand merchandise they are trying to foist on the public as "the canned sauerkraut of Spengler's 'Prussian Socialism,' the commonplaces of the Wasteland outlook, the cheap mental stimulants of Alienation." Finally, to insure their never having a market for their wares, Herzog casts aspersions on the middle-class consumers of such damaged goods. One explanation Herzog offers for their gullibility is that their lives have grown so safe and tedious that they are quick to purchase any thrills, no matter how contrived or injurious they might be. Because they have not had many opportunities to witness firsthand "apocalypses, fires, drownings, stranglings, and the rest of it," they attempt to satisfy their craving for the lurid by reading about the cataclysmic decine of the West, the ghastly void, and the fall into the terrifying quotidian. The other explanation Herzog suggests for the bourgeoisie's fascination with morbid ideas is similar to the one Diana Trilling furnishes: since the view of life as absurd has been highly endorsed by the best philosophical and literary circles, "to subscribe to this particular vision . . . is unmistakably to qualify for membership in a cultural elite" (*Claremont Essays*). Herzog evidently has this in mind when he wittily remarks, "Literate people appropriate all the best things they can find in books, and dress themselves in them just as certain crabs are supposed to beautify themselves with seaweed." Frantically striving to be intellectually fashionable, to be at one with their cultural betters, they pretend to be crisis-ridden, alienated, and desperate. Indeed, Herzog underscores the inanity of having desperation as a prerequisite for belonging to the privileged class by hyperbolically commenting, "The day is fast approaching . . . when only proof that you are despairing will entitle you to the vote, instead of the means test, the pole tax, the literacy exam."

Along with making sport of the overrated angst of the spurious cognoscenti and those aspiring to join their ranks, Herzog ridicules the recent unwholesome preoccupation with death. The particular necrophiles he attacks are those German existentialists who lecture that "God is no more. But Death is." If man would only lingeringly contemplate death, they claim, he would be rescued from distraction, gain freedom, and become "authentic." Herzog finds such a view nonsensical and dismisses it as another variation of "the old *memento mori,* the monk's skull on the table, brought up to date." This is not to say that he objects to man's facing up to his mortality. Unlike Augie, who only fleetingly alludes to death in his euphoric disquisitions, or Henderson, who tries to avoid its imminence with acrobatic zeal, Herzog has reconciled himself to his eventual passing. Without such a reconciliation, he believes that the human spirit, "racing and conniving to evade death . . . holds its breath and hopes to be immortal because it does not live." But Herzog cannot accept the "notion that a practiced and deliberate confrontation with death and despair will lead man to greater human depth" (Donald Markos). The intentional courting of death, that is, purposely "disintegrating ourselves by our own wills in proof of our 'freedom,' " is, in his opinion, the worst kind of folly rather than the best kind of wisdom. The alternative he proposes is "acknowledging that we owe a human life to this waking spell of existence, regardless of the void." Rather than practicing "over-kill" on ourselves, we would have time for the most meaningful task of all: "our employment by other human beings and their employment by us."

Similarly, Herzog looks askance at the current adulation of suffering for its own sake. Unlike Malamud's heroes who define themselves through their experiences with sorrow and obtain a certain ecstasy through agony, it is a sign of Herzog's emotional recovery that he can relinquish the harrowing for the halcyon. As he sees it, the only kind of people who benefit from adversity are the truly religious, because they use it as an "opportunity to experience evil and change it into good." But for the majority of people suffering is not in the least ennobling. If anything, it robs them of their dignity and blunts their sensitivity. To say that suffering is the necessary "antidote to illusion" is to spout a vacuous cocktail party expression. Herzog realizes that man will inevitably experience his fair share of pain through the course of a lifetime, so it is utterly ridiculous to "expound suffering for anyone or call for Hell to make us serious and truthful."

Closely related to Herzog's mockery of the recent obsession with despair, death, and suffering is his diatribe against modern cynicism. Like the prophet Amos, lamenting the fall of the "virgin Israel . . . with none to raise her up," he upbraids this generation for thinking "that nothing faithful, vulnerable, fragile can be durable or have any true power." In the novel the principal advocates of this cynical view are Herzog's legal advisers, Simkin and Himmelstein, who, to use the words of Oscar Wilde, "know the price of everything and the value of nothing." For them as well as for Augie's "Machiavellians," the world is populated not with honest men, but with "whores." Nobility, sincerity, and goodness do not exist. Only the "nasty" constitutes the real, or, as Herzog trenchantly reduces their perverted code to its most ludicrous extreme: "You must sacrifice your poor, squawking, niggardly individuality . . . to historical necessity. And to truth. And truth is true only as it brings down more disgrace and dreariness upon human beings, so that if it shows anything except evil it is illusion, and not truth." Appointing themselves Herzog's "Reality Instructors," Simkin and Himmelstein continually blast away at him with their truth and insist that he accept their "brutal version of the . . . American way of life." Herzog refuses to become their pupil, however. He still has faith that even in the twentieth century one can "live in an inspired condition." Like Augie, he believes there can be "Man, with a capital *M*, with great stature." Herzog disregards those "snarling realists" and ends up viewing them merely as grotesque characters in the currently running "drama of disease, of self-revenge" in "an age of special comedy."

These are just a few of the ideas which Herzog's nimble wit has played with. As Tony Tanner has indicated, "[All of] Herzog's thoughts and concerns are too various to summarize; indeed their profuse, unrelated multiplicity is an essential part of the meaning of the book." But from the sampling that has been presented it is very apparent that, until Artur Sammler, Herzog is Bellow's most deft "vaudevillian of the mind" who is able to amuse his audience with both obvious and subtle intellectual comedy (Robert Shulman).

As one of those humanists who have dedicated themselves to the "struggle toward suitable words," Herzog has a ready talent for verbal humor. He generally knows which words precisely convey his serious intentions and which ones humorously camouflage them. He can draft sentences of great profundity and great parody. He can employ phrases which flatter his ego and those which deflate it. Moreover, each time he tampers with language to trivialize his concerns and minimize his achievements, he not only amuses himself with his clever distortions, but he changes our perspective as well. His rhetorical twists upset our expectations and compel us to reassess him and his insights. In the process we laugh at his verbal deviations and perceive new shifts of meaning which we would not have had if Herzog had not taken any liberties with language. We see this technique best in Herzog's bastardization of quotations. A master of sleight-of-word, he produces ingenious adaptations of popular and erudite lines to mock and modify his behavior. For example, he both spoofs and stresses his masochistic tendencies by changing Emerson's "Hitch your wagon to a star" to his own "Hitch your agony to a star." Guilt-ridden over his purchase of pagan clothing and his flight to hedonistic Martha's Vineyard, he both ridicules and underscores his frailty by parodying the Lord's Prayer: "O Lord! . . . forgive all these trespasses. Lead me not into Penn Station." He also employs his antic coinages to reprove others. Upset by the disappearance of privacy in American life, he comes up with his own sardonic variation of Gresham's Law: "Bad money drives out good." Herzog's amended law, which is equally astute, reads, "Public life drives out private life." He expresses his enmity for Valentine by playfully suggesting how such an intellectual faker might pervert Martin Buber's words. "Maybe [Valentine] wants to swap wives with a rabbi. He'll work his way round from 'I and Thou' to 'Me and You'—'You and Me, Kid!' " Herzog gives vent to his hatred of Madeleine by splicing two commonplace adages, "A stitch in time saves nine," and "Familiarity breeds contempt," thereby originating his own satiric portmanteau maxim: "A bitch in time breeds contempt." Herzog's mongrelized expressions amuse us with their unusual combination of hackneyed strains and increase our understanding of the principal concerns of the novel through their unexpected emphases.

In addition to fragmenting and reconstructing quotations for comic effect, Herzog takes well-known quotations out of context and introduces them in the context of his narration. While they give evidence of Herzog's amazingly fertile and retentive mind, they initially appear entirely inappropriate and irrelevant to the proceedings at hand. But upon reconsideration and by a wild stretch of the imagination, they are in some respects fitting and even contribute an added dimension to our interpretation of character and situation. As for the other respects in which they are incongruously out of place and hyperbolically ungermane to what is going on, they provide us with whimsical relief from the woeful. For example, Herzog, overwhelmed with a mass of intellectual and household chores, turns his plight into mock tragedy by melodramatically citing a Latin translation of a line from Euripides: "*Quos vult perdere dementat* [Whom God wills to destroy he first makes mad]." He wryly exposes his penchant for luxuriating in sorrow by quoting the Johnsonian epigram, "Grief, Sir, is a species of idleness." He makes his vindictiveness toward Madeleine and Valentine appear ridiculously excessive by uttering the same curse against them which the Hebrews reserved for their most vile enemies, the Amalekites: "*Yemach sh'mo!* Let their names be blotted out!" He points up the absurdity of his trying to become a genuine New Englander by quoting with tongue in cheek the sententious line from Robert Frost's Kennedy inaugural poem, "The Gift Outright": "The land was ours before we were the land's." He causes us to laugh about the homosexual assault he received as a child. Shortly after describing it in awful detail, he recalls the passages from the New Testament which "the good Christian lady" read to him in the hospital: "Suffer the little children to come unto me," and "Give and it shall be given unto you. Good measure . . . shall men give into your bosom." By exhuming such quotations long buried in Herzog's consciousness and having them interrupt his thoughts at the most unlikely yet apt times, Bellow undercuts Herzog's troubles by casting them within mirth-provoking frames of reference.

Herzog uses allusions in much the same way. Since he is adept at juggling a wide assortment of ideas, he is equally adept at tossing out a great variety of allusions. Unlike Augie March, his aim is not to show off the breadth of his knowledge. More certain of his intellectual endowments than his newly learned predecessor, he does not frenetically muster into active duty all the allusions at his command. He calls into play only those which could conceivably refer to his own life, yet at the same time are the most preposterously unlike his own life. He thereby enables us to see him in a newer light because of the chain of associations which his imaginative allusions have set in motion. He simultaneously makes himself more ludicrous because of the farfetched comparisons he does make. By dubbing himself a "patient Griselda," the adoring wife in Chaucer's "Clerk's Tale" who remained faithful to her husband even though he took away her children and pretended to remarry, Herzog emphasizes how idiotic he was to endure Madeleine's cruel treatment of him for such a long time. By admitting that he intended to become the "Lovejoy" of his generation, Herzog makes fun of his intellectual presumptions. By referring to his "Faustian spirit of discontent," he ridicules his sudden concern for "social questions . . . the external world" when all along he had been hibernating in his private world of books. By calling his Berkshire retreat "Herzog's folly," he humorously links his imprudent acquisition to Seward's shrewd purchase of Alaska. And when he surveys the ruins of his estate, he mock-heroically compares himself to Shelley's Ozymandias, the Egyptian pharaoh whose mighty kingdom decayed beyond recognition in the desert sands. To be sure, Herzog realizes that he falls short of the illustrious personages with whom he facetiously claims kinship. Yet these facetious claims allow him to escape momentarily from "the agony of consciousness and separate being." By comically relating himself to universal figures, he can move beyond his own dilemma and see it with some detachment.

Herzog aims his most deprecating allusions at the chief traitors of the camp—Valentine and Madeleine. By pointing up their similarity to the least admirable and their dissimilarity to the most admirable men of the past, he gets his verbal revenge. By likening Valentine to Cagliostro, the eighteenth-century Italian charlatan who pretended to be a noble and duped the credulous with his feats of alchemy and magic, Herzog comically accentuates Valentine's spuriousness. Conversely, by referring to Valentine as a *Shofat*, a judge in ancient Israel noted for being a supremely righteous man and a charismatic leader, Herzog points up Valentine's ludicrously deficient portrayal of the role. Madeleine is damned with the same kind of perverted praise. By suggesting that she expects to give birth to a Louis XIV since she purchases a five-hundred-dollar maternity outfit, Herzog ridicules her delusions of royalty and her habitual prodigality. By contrasting her with the Duke of Wellington, "the victor of Waterloo [who] drew apart to shed bitter tears" for his slain enemies, Herzog mordantly stresses how uncompassionately Madeleine treats him, her vanquished foe.

Herzog directs his barbs at less offensive parties as well, although it is not his intention to injure them seriously. He simply enjoys amusing himself by mildly grazing their weak spots. By observing that the pedant Shapiro combs his hair "in the Rudolph Valentino" style, he waggishly indicates the incongruity of such a "dumpy"-looking creature straining to appear the glamorous figure. By describing his brother Shura as a "true disciple of Thomas Hobbes," who asks "nothing better than to prosper in the belly of Leviathan," Herzog makes light of Shura's opportunism. By referring to his Ludeyville neighbors as "Jukes and Kallikaks," the feeble-minded and morally degenerate families studied by sociologists at the end of the nineteenth century, Herzog playfully exaggerates his neighbors' mental obtuseness and moral laxity. Even the benevolent Ramona does not escape Herzog's raillery. By ironically calling her "a priestess of Isis," the Egyptian fertility goddess, he reveals her elaborate worship of Eros to be a highly developed form of nonsense.

Along with employing allusions to divert and distance himself from his anguish, Herzog is an expert at verbal retrieval. Since he is the most articulate of the Bellow heroes mentioned thus far and experiences the keenest sense of outrage, he originates the most ingenious "verbal phrases and kinetic metaphors with which suffering man escalates implacable defeats into comic impasses" (Earl Rovit, *Saul Bellow*). Herzog ruefully jests, for example, about the misery he endures as a result of Madeleine's encroaching intellectualism. "She's built a wall of Russian books around herself. Vladimir of Kiev, Tikhon Zadonsky. In my bed! It's not enough they persecuted my ancestors!" He hyperbolically likens Madeleine's traits of paranoia, whose effects he has suffered, to the ten plagues visited upon the Egyptians. He laughs bitterly at the fact that he has been chosen to be the butt of Madeleine's wrath. "It would not be practical for her to hate herself. Luckily, God sends a substitute, a husband." A frequent victim of female treachery in general, he expresses his misogyny in the caustic quip, "What do [women] want? They eat green salad and drink human blood." Herzog "doggedly persists in twisting a smile . . . under the grip of . . . adversity" (Earl Rovit, "Bernard Malamud and the Jewish Literary Tradition," *Critique* 3 [1960]), while his astringent wit permits him to take the sting out of that adversity.

In addition to his verbal retrievals, Herzog is a man of letters. The epistles of Moses, however, are not always gospel. Like Bummidge in *The Last Analysis*, he is "earnest when he is clowning and clowning when he means to be earnest." Yet Herzog's portfolio includes not only soberly foolish and foolishly sober correspondence. He dashes off conciliatory and antagonistic, naive and sophisticated, petty and magnanimous letters. His other literary accomplishments include giving a "Great Books course" to Nehru, Churchill, and Eisenhower, improvising whimsical children's stories, composing an "Insect Iliad," and reciting charming nursery rhymes. He is equally adept at drawing satiric vignettes of those he detests and idealized portraits of those he loves. He is able to rattle off rarefied abstractions and dignified biblical Hebrew, as well as colorful ghetto Yiddishisms and off-color gutter Americanisms. Herzog is a skilled wordsmith who forges many kinds of language which, when rubbed against each other, throw off the sparks of verbal comedy.

Herzog's utterances are drolly voluble as well as drolly versatile. Like Wilhelm and Henderson, Herzog "has a compulsion to tell all, to overtell, to explain all, to explain away" (Stanley Edgar Hyman). Indeed, Ramona calls attention to this particular compulsion: "What is funny is how completely you answer any question." Herzog is also aware of how funny his "strict and literal truthfulness" is; yet he cannot stop revealing the whole truth about himself, no matter how uncomplimentary it may be. We receive a detailed account of his poor grooming habits, his absentmindedness, his physical ailments, his social faux pas, his sexual victories and defeats. Herzog is even more garrulous when discussing intellectual matters. As he himself observes, "People legislate continually by means of talk." He, too, is bursting with pronouncements and believes that the only way he can exert his authority is by inundating reality with his language. Hence he is compelled to be always in the "full flood of discourse" (Malcolm Bradbury, "Saul Bellow and the Naturalist Tradition," *Review of English Literature* 4 [1963]): "Quickly, quickly, more! . . . Herzog . . . felt his eager, flying spirit streaming out, speaking, piercing, making clear judgements, uttering final explanations, necessary words only." But by the end of the novel Herzog feels that such judgments and explanations are no longer necessary. Having served his sentence of wracking cogitation, he no longer has "to control the world with words and ideas" and can "live unencumbered as another creature in the world that is" (John J. Clayton). And so we leave Herzog with his spell of intense consciousness at an end and his jocosely profuse words temporarily silenced.

Herzog does not possess the range of comedy that exists in *The Adventures of Augie March* and *Henderson the Rain King*. Although it does capture the rueful mirth of Herzog's corporeal imperfections obstructing his bids for spiritual perfection, it does not contain the humor of the body worsted in unusual physical action, nor does it reveal that body caught up in a rash of preposterous situations. It is primarily what was said of *Tristram Shandy*, that "history book . . . of what passes in a man's mind." Throughout most of the novel we are in Herzog's mind, observing not his physical, but his mental pratfalls. This is not to say that Bellow wants to stifle our admiration for Herzog's extraordinary speculative powers; these powers catapult him into all spheres of the learned domain and are responsible for generating his all-inclusive ideological comedy. But what Bellow proves to be ridiculous is Herzog's presumption that he can intellectually resolve all of the complex issues of his age, or at least control his environment solely through an intellectual awareness of it. Moreover, Bellow illustrates the folly of Herzog's grasping at lofty ideas to avoid coping with his own problems, and his clinging to childish views of reality which prevent a mature confrontation with it. Yet despite Herzog's mental pratfalls, he does manage through hard-won insight and gratuitous intuition to regain his equilibrium. Having employed his rapier wit for both self-dissection and salvation, he is able to make the steadiest gesture of comic affirmation of Bellow's euphoric heroes. Unlike Augie March, who can never be still enough to locate his "axial lines," or Henderson, who can never stop "making such a noise" in order to "hear something nice," Herzog is no longer compelled "to enact the peculiarities of life," and can accept his limited condition. Having "broken out of [his] own skull," he is "ready to break into other skulls." At the novel's end, however, we find him in his Eden communing only with God and nature. His privacy as yet uninvaded and his newfound tranquility as yet undisturbed, he awaits the arrival of another human being.

Herzog, or, Bellow in Trouble

Richard Poirier

Bellow's most important cultural essays—"The Thinking Man's Waste-land" (1965), his talk to the PEN Conference in 1966 (as it later appeared in *The New York Times Book Review*), and, in 1971, "Culture Now: Some Animadversions, Some Laughs"—address themselves directly, and with often startling crudity of mind, to the cultural issues which came to dominate his fiction after *Seize the Day*. In particular, *Herzog* in 1964 and *Mr. Sammler's Planet* in 1968 are efforts to test out, to substantiate, to vitalize, and ultimately to propagate a kind of cultural conservatism which he shares with the two aggrieved heroes of these novels, and to imagine that they are victims of the cultural debasements, as Bellow sees it, of the sixties.

The fact that some of his best work—*The Victim, Dangling Man,* and *Seize the Day*—are generally regarded as distinguished contributions to the literature of the Waste Land tradition would not in itself invalidate his disparagements of that tradition or of the academic promotion of it. Other writers, including Mailer, have managed to live within some such complex of attitudes to their own and to our profit. The difference in Mailer's case is that he has a confidently zestful appetite for, and an assurance in his capacities to cope with, the cultural obscenities which might otherwise force him into those feelings of self-righteous victimization so crippling to Bellow's work. Without knowing it, Bellow is far more alienated than Mailer. It shows in his writing; or rather in the evidence that the act of

---

From *Saul Bellow: A Collection of Critical Essays,* edited by Earl Rovit. © 1975 by Prentice-Hall, Inc., Englewood Cliffs, New Jersey.

writing, and the promise of cultural mastery which might be engendered by it, is not in his case sufficient to save him from the feelings of victimization visited on his heroes. And yet he likes continually to imagine that it is. Thus when he speaks out in the PEN address against "the disaffected, subversive, radical clique," he doesn't seem to recognize there, anymore than in his novels, that he is exposing his own "disaffection," poorly disguised by bad jokes:

> On the one hand these teachers, editors, or cultural bureaucrats have absorbed the dislike of modern classic writers for modern civilization. They are repelled by the effrontery of power, and the degradation of the urban crowd. They have made the Waste Land outlook their own. On the other hand they are very well off. They have money, position, privileges, power. They send their children to private schools. They can afford elegant dental care, jet holidays in Europe. They have stocks, bonds, houses, even yachts. With all this, owing to their education, they enjoy a particular and intimate sympathy with the heroic artistic life. Their tastes and judgments were formed by Rimbaud and D. H. Lawrence. Could anything be neater?

There is a random vulgarity in the superficial notations of this passage which is but one evidence of Bellow's effort to blind himself to the fact that he is no less "repelled" by such things as "the degradation of the urban crowd." This has been, after all, a theme in all his work; it is responsible for some of its most powerful descriptive efforts; and one is forced into the embarrassment of supposing that the essential difference between Bellow and the people he is here criticizing is that he, but not they, deserves "elegant dental care," etc., etc., etc. Bellow's problem in the sixties is that the imagined forces of dissolution are not, in this passage or elsewhere in his writing during the period, substantially enough evoked, are indeed too trivially evoked, to teach him, in Empson's phrase, "a style from a despair."

Despite some surface differences, the style of *Herzog* and of *Mr. Sammler's Planet* projects the same authorial presence: of a man nursing imagined betrayals, a man who chooses to retaliate by historical pontifications which, given his own sense of the wastes of history, are intellectually barren, and who nonetheless tries to validate what he says by a species of comic evasion. The comedy, that is, is a way of convincing us that because he himself presumably knows he's being rhetorically banal, the banality must therefore illustrate not the deprivations of his imagination but the bankruptcy of contemporary culture. No one who does not hopelessly confuse culture with literature and both of these with the limits set by the accomplishments of Saul Bellow is apt to be convinced by this procedure.

The test is all in the "doing," as James said long ago, and it is peculiar that those who share Bellow's cultural conservatism have failed to ask themselves whether or not his performance as a writer, as distinct from his opinions as a would-be thinker, contribute to the vitalization either of literary culture or the language. On any close inspection, Bellow's rhetorical ambitions are seen to be disjointed from those aspects of his later fiction which are most compelling—the brilliance of detailed, especially of grotesque, portraiture, and a genius for the rendering of Yiddish-American speech. In *Herzog* in particular, his writing is most alive when he writes as a kind of local colorist. And yet, in the language of analysis and Big Thinking with which he endows his hero, and it is, again, of a piece with the canting style of Bellow's essays, he wants to be taken as a novelist of civilization, especially the civilization of cultural degeneracy as it affects the urban-centered Jew in the American sixties.

That he tries to localize these immense concerns within essentially Jewish material is not the problem. After all, the Jewish writer in the American city is potentially as well situated within the tensions of a great cultural conflict as was Faulkner in the Mississippi of the Snopses, the Faulkner of the middle period when he was writing out of what a similarly beleaguered writer—Yeats in Ireland—called his "ill luck." Bellow feels threatened in his role as public defender of two distinct yet historically harmonious cultural inheritances: of the Jew as poor immigrant, the outsider whose native resources save him from the bitterness of alienation, and of the Jew as successful *arriviste* in American society, enriched and burdened all at once by traditions of high culture. Now a kind of insider looking out, he yearns for those cultural supports which, since World War II, have been commercialized by the society at large if not submerged entirely under the tidal waves of mass produced taste. All differences allowed, a similar combination of inheritances is precisely what fired the genius of Faulkner and Lawrence and Yeats, all of whom were also at the crossroads where high and what might be called native culture find themselves both threatened and courted by the commercialized culture of the middle.

This is a difficult position for a writer to be in; it is also an extraordinarily profitable one. Bellow has so far shown himself unequal to them. Because if contemporary culture is so corrupt and corrupting as he makes it out to be, then the very rhetoric he so glibly uses in his essays and in the essayistic meditations of Herzog and Sammler is more discredited than he dares admit. In the writings of this century where there is a disposition about the state of the culture similar to Bellow's, there is also a kind of stylistic and formal complication generally missing from his work. This complication is not "academic" or faddish or willful. Instead it reflects a confirmed sense of the enormous effort required both to include, with any kind of human generosity, and then to correct, by the powers of style, the preponderant influences of pop culture and of a ruined education system. Some of the consequences to Bellow's work of the essential timidity of his effort—like all timidity it tends to be both self-pitying and vindictive— have been noticed by Morris Dickstein and Richard Locke and by a few of the reviewers of *Mr. Sammler's Planet*. But *Herzog*, while being universally praised, was nonetheless equally flawed, an indication of what was later to become more evidently the matter.

With what Bellow tells brilliantly, the career of Herzog, many are probably now familiar: a twice married sometime professor of English, author of *Romanticism and Christianity* and of a child in each of his marriages, Herzog has recently been divorced, at 47, by his second wife Madeleine. She, in his recollections, shows unusual competence in disposing of her body, other people's ideas, and Herzog's schedule, thus taking, unobserved, his best friend and confidant, Valentine Gersbach, to her bed. It is a story of betrayals, and of a mind so fevered that it remembers them with an attention luridly bright and constantly shifting: to his lawyer, to his psychiatrists, to his colleagues, to his family, to his various women, especially Ramona, middle-ageing, generous, loveable and nonetheless made a bit ridiculous, as is everyone in Herzog's account except children and a few other minor characters. Everything we know about these people we know from Herzog's mind. They are confined to the jumble of his recollections as he lies alone in the run-down house he bought for Madeleine in the Berkshires, cheated in this, too. He returns there at the end of the novel, which is also the conclusion of the actions about which he begins to reminisce on page one. The enclosed, self-protective quality of the book is thus formally sealed: its end is its beginning.

Given Bellow's ambitions so much to exceed the confined circumstances of his hero's life and to make it a "representative" modern one, his method seems, on the very face of it, disastrously claustrophobic. Normally we'd wonder how the author is to operate freely within such a book, much less manage to puff it up. Of course he makes himself felt in the ordering of things, so that the fragments of the story as they flash through Herzog's mind are comically, sometimes critically juxtaposed with his intellectual theorizings. And the very first line, "If I am out of my mind, it's all right with me, thought Moses Herzog," is a joke about the hero's "rightness" and about his "thinking" that maybe we're expected to carry like a comic tuning fork through the rest of the book. The evidence increases as one reads, however, that Bellow is in the novel whenever he wants to be simply by becoming Herzog, the confusions at many points between the narrative "I" and "he" being a blunt and even attractive admission of this. But the identification of hero and author is apparent in other, ultimately more insidious ways. Thus Herzog is allowed to characterize himself in a manner usually reserved to the objectivity of the author: the letters he writes, and never mails, to the living who betrayed his love, to the dead thinkers who betray his thinking, to the living great who betray him politically are, he says, "ridiculous." (He does not himself betray the book by also admitting that the letters, for all the parroted praise the reviews have given them, are frequently uninventive and tiresome.) He claims also not to like his own personality.

Bellow's novelist skill is here seen most adroitly at the service of his larger intellectual and, too obviously, of his more personal motives. Allowing no version of the alleged betrayals other than Herzog's, Bellow still must protect his hero's claims to guiltlessness by a process all the more ultimately effective for being paradoxical: he lets Herzog's suffering issue forth less as accusations against others than as self-contempt for his having been cozened by them. There could be no more effective way to disarm the reader's scepticism about the confessions of such a hero within so protective a narrative form. Bellow can thus operate snugly (and smugly) within the enclosure of his hero's recollections, assured, at least to his own satisfaction, that he has anticipated and therefore forestalled antagonistic intrusions from outside. He really does want Herzog's mind to be the whole world, and the hero's ironies at his own expense are only his cleverest ruse in the arrangement. No wonder, then, that Herzog's talk about himself and about ideas is, in passages that carry great weight, indistinguishable from the generalized Bellovian rhetoric by which here, as in Bellow's other novels, "victims" become "modern man," their situation the World's: "He saw his perplexed, furious eyes and he gave an audible cry. *My God! Who is this creature? It considers itself human. But what is it? Not human in itself. But it has the longing to be human.*"

The recurrence of such passages in Bellow's work is only one indication of how straight we are to take them, of how much he tends to summarize himself in the pseudo-philosophical or sociological or historical expansions of the otherwise parochial situations of his heroes. Perhaps the most lamentable result of Bellow's complicity at such points is that he loses his customary ear for banality of expression or for the fatuity of the sentiments. I don't know another writer equally talented who surrenders so willingly to what are by now platitudes about his own creations. Seldom in Faulkner, even less in Joyce, and far less frequently in Lawrence than people who can't listen to his prose like to believe, do we find what the literary ragpickers call key passages. Where such passages obtrude in writing that asks us to be discriminating about style, as they do in Fitzgerald and Hemingway as well as in Bellow, there is always a lack of assurance in what Bellow has himself called "the sole source of order in art": the "power of imagination." And he distinguished this from "the order that ideas have." "Critics need to be reminded of this," he remarks in "Distractions of a Fiction Writer."

His alertness in the matter is understandable. Between his evident intellectual ambitions and the fictional materials he thinks congenial to them there is in *Herzog*, as in *Henderson the Rain King* and in *The Adventures of Augie March*, a gap across which these novels never successfully move. Sections of the present book read like a lesser *Middlemarch*, the longest of the "ridiculous" letters offering pretty much what Bellow-Herzog want to say about "modern" life. Herzog's interest in Romanticism is itself an expression of a familiar concern of Bellow: the effort to preserve individuality during a period of economic and scientific acceleration with which it is supposedly impossible for the human consciousness to keep pace. Henry Adams, among others, gave us the vocabulary; George Eliot predicted the condition; Bellow the novelist is victimized by it. What I call the gap in his novels between their intellectual and historical pretensions, on one side, and the stuff of life as he renders it, on the other, prevents me from believing that he is himself convinced by his snappy contempt for "the commonplaces of the Waste Land outlook, the cheap mental stimulants of Alienation." Quoted from a letter of Herzog's these are obviously identical with Bellow's own attitudes. My objection isn't merely that Bellow would replace the "commonplaces" of alienation with even more obvious commonplaces about "the longing to be human." I mean that his works, the truest and surest direction of their energy, suggest to me that imaginatively Bellow does not himself find a source of order in these commonplaces.

Lawrence, who would have found Bellow interesting, was right: "Never trust the artist. Trust the tale. The proper function of the critic is to save the tale from the artist who created it." Imagine such a critic's response to Bellow's connivance at his hero's self-promotion as Your Ordinary Striver:

Just then his state of being was so curious that he was compelled, himself, to see it—eager, grieving, fantastic, dangerous,
crazed and, to the point of death, "comical." It was enough to
make a man pray to God to remove this great, bone-breaking
burden of selfhood and self-development, give himself, a failure, back to the species for a primitive cure. But this was becoming the up-to-date and almost conventional way of looking
at any single life. In this view the body itself, with its two arms
and vertical length, was compared to the Cross, on which you
knew the agony of consciousness and separate being. For that
matter, he had been taking this primitive cure, administered by
Madeleine, Sandor, et cetera; so that his recent misfortunes
might be seen as a collective project, himself participating, to
destroy his vanity and his pretensions to a personal life so that
he might disintegrate and suffer and hate like so many others,
not on anything so distinguished as a cross, but down in the
mire of post-Renaissance, post-humanistic, post-Cartesian dissolution, next door to the Void. Everybody was in the act.
"History" gave everyone a free ride. The very Himmelsteins,
who had never even read a book of metaphysics, were touting
the Void as if it were so much salable real estate. This little demon was impregnated with modern ideas, and one in particular
excited his terrible little heart; you must sacrifice your poor,
squawking, niggardly individuality—which may be nothing
anyway (from an analytic viewpoint) but a persistent infant
megalomania, or (from a Marxian point of view) a stinking little bourgeois property—to historical necessity. And to truth.
And truth is true only as it brings down more disgrace and
dreariness upon human beings, so that if it shows anything except evil it is illusion, and not truth. But of course he, Herzog,
predictably bucking such trends, had characteristically, obsti-
nately, defiantly, blindly but without sufficient courage or intelligence tried to be a *marvelous* Herzog, a Herzog who,
perhaps clumsily, tried to live out marvelous qualities vaguely
comprehended.

Though Bellow is among the most intelligent of contemporary American writers, I can't find in this glib presumption to Thought any difference between his and Herzog's presence. Distinction of intellect is of
course not necessary to fiction; but what is most bothersome about the

passage is Bellow's failure to acknowledge the comic preposterousness of the kind of mental activity going on in it, a pretension that might itself characterize the hero were he not at this point indistinguishable from the author. Nothing but nothing in Herzog's career—are we to think of his surrender of his wife's diaphragm to her messenger Gersbach?—suggests that his selfhood or self-development has been "this great bone-breaking burden." Such terms describe nothing in the book. They refer instead to a literary historical commonplace about the self to which Bellow wants his book attached. "Species," "primitive cure"—the vocabulary continues to mythologize a life that has been shown to be at most pitiably insipid. Typically, even the effort at inflation gets blamed on the times: Herzog abuses himself for thinking in a way so "up-to-date and almost conventional." When does it end! Betrayed by someone in the way he thinks of how someone has betrayed him! Having therefore rejected a place on the Cross (actually by 1964 so worn a piece of literary furniture as to be ready, like Art Nouveau, for sentimental revival) he momentarily settles "down in the mire of post-Renaissance, post-humanistic, post-Cartesian dissolution, next door to the Void." Alas, another neighborhood too fashionable for honest H. The process of correction and mockery by which these successive placements are given up involves, of course, the wholly unacceptable assumption that the novel has made Herzog in some way suitable for them. Not every hero in modern literature is allowed uncritically to try on for size so many distinguished roles and then to say not that they don't fit but that they are too much in season. By the end of the passage Herzog is our culture hero "predictably bucking such trends," though how, where, with whom and in what sense he does any "bucking," how he might even ironically call himself "marvelous Herzog," the things that happen in the novel and that get said in it, this passage being a sample, don't and cannot show. Yes, the terms of the passage are those of an English professor whose book is being stolen from him as mysteriously (if you think like Herzog) as was his wife. But they are also Bellow's terms despite his little ironies, Audenesque in the double take of their direction. What is missing is any indication that Bellow is aware of the *essential* irrelevance, the *essential* pretension and shabbiness of the self-aggrandizing mind at work in, and for, the hero.

To a considerable degree the novel does work as a rather conventional drama of alienation, though this is precisely what Bellow doesn't want it to be. It is about the failure of all available terms for interpretation and summary, about the intellectual junk heap of language by which Herzog-Bellow propose dignities to the hero's life and then as quickly watch these proposals dissolve into cliché. A similar process goes on in *Augie,* against the competition of an anxious and often phony exuberance, and it was there that Bellow began to fashion a comic prose which could bear the simultaneous weight of cultural, historical, mythological evocations and also sustain the exposure of their irrelevance. His comedy always has in it the penultimate question before the final one, faced in *Seize the Day,* of life or death—the question of what can be taken seriously and how seriously it can possibly be taken. The result, however, is a kind of stalemate achieved simply by not looking beyond the play of humor into its constituents, at the person from whom it issues, at the psychological implications both of anyone's asking such questions and of the *way* in which he asks them.

It seems to me that Bellow cannot break the stalemate with alienation implicit in his comedy without surrendering to the Waste Land outlook and foregoing the mostly unconvincing rhetoric which he offers as an alternative. That is why his comic style in *Herzog,* even more than in *Henderson* or *Augie,* is less like Nathanael West's than like that of West's brother-in-law, S. J. Perelman. Both Perelman and Bellow raise the question of "seriousness" by piling up trivial detail, by their mock submission to the cheery hope of redemption that people find in the ownership of certain "things," in certain styles, in certain totemic phrases: "I am thirty-eight years old," begins one of Perelman's sketches, "have curly brown hair and blue eyes, own a uke and a yellow roadster, and am considered a snappy dresser in my crowd. But the thing I want most in the world for my birthday is a free subscription to *Oral Hygiene,* published by Merwin B. Massol, 1005 Liberty Avenue, Pittsburgh, Pa." And in another piece, to the remark of a West Indian maid, "You mus' be crazy," he allows the reply " 'But aren't we all?' I reminded her with a charming smile. *'C'est la maladie du temps*—the sickness of the times—don't you think? *Fin-de-siècle* and lost generation in a way.' " Compare to the first Herzog's purchases of summer garb or Ramona's dedication to shrimp Arnaud, New Orleans style; compare to the second a lot of Herzog's intellectualizing; and for an equivalent to Perelman's high "theatric" mode see Madeleine's bitch performance when she makes her switches "into the slightly British diction [Herzog] had learned to recognize as a sure sign of trouble."

Bellow has greatly increased the range of such comedy, from the clutter of "things," a post-Depression comedy, to the clutter of ideas and culture, a comedy after affluence. But he is still anxious to stay within that comedy. He doesn't dare ask any questions about it or about the characters from whom it emerges. That's why the comparison to Perelman is an apt one. And I mean no criticism of Perelman, whose intentions are not those of a novelist, particularly of novelist-as-thinker. I mean to say that Bellow's failure to ask tough questions about where he *himself* wants to be taken seriously, a failure of his ruined recent play, *The Last Analysis*, doesn't allow me to take him seriously when he chooses to talk about Herzog's struggle for self-development or when, after the scene in court, he allows reference to "the unbearable intensity of these ideas." In question are such ideas as: "If the old God exists he must be a murderer. But the one true God is death." Sophomoric tag-lines don't deserve the status of "ideas." Whatever they are they're really as comfortable as old shoes, especially when you can so believe in their "unbearable intensity" that you can lie down. And it is from that position that the story is told.

Bellow and Freud

Daniel Fuchs

Like many writers and intellectuals of his generation, Bellow was genuinely involved with psychoanalysis. "Off the couch by Christmas" was a common hope or familiar joke in literary circles. Bellow himself tried a variety of approaches stemming from Freud and Reich. "I've had all the psychiatry I can use," Moses Herzog tells Dr. Emmerich. Though much has been made of his switch from Freud to Reich, Bellow's connection with the utopian Reich was short-lived. Freud was the more enduring presence, the genius of psychoanalysis, the therapeutic and ideational father for whom Bellow expressed the inevitable love-hate. He has learned from Freud but essentially opposes him. To say that Bellow knows Freud very well is no exaggeration. There was a period when Freud was his nightly bedtime reading, and Bellow's frequent references to Freud in his fictive works, his notebooks, and his essays reveal an easy intimacy not only with major works but also with minor ones. As for the legitimacy of comparing an artist with a thinker, few thinkers have had more to do with "vision" than Freud, few novelists more to do with the meaning and emotional content of ideas than Bellow. Freud saw all systems of thought, including his own, as mythology. And the Bellow protagonist often breathes in what Bellow, in his spoof of Freud, has called "an environment of Ideas" (*The Last Analysis,* [all further references to this text will be abbreviated as *LA*]).

From *Studies in the Literary Imagination* 17, no. 2 (Fall 1984). © 1984 by the Department of English, George State University.

Moreover, Bellow does not encounter in Freud an arcane scientist or offbeat mind. Freudian perceptions are at the heart of twentieth-century life. Freud gives us a view of man which is new, denuding, disillusioned, which is radically subjective and iconoclastic, which is, in short, modern. Bellow's resistance to Freud begins in opposition to the terms with which these views are given. Freud is a prime instance of modernism, against which Bellow has mounted a sustained critique.

"I didn't want to be what he called determined," says Augie March (*The Adventures of Augie March,* [all further references to this text will be abbreviated as *AM*]). He is thinking here of the environmental determinism warned against by Einhorn and extending it to a defense of personal autonomy, a goal that he or anyone else can only partially achieve. Though fully aware of the forces that oppose it, he insists on the reality of autonomy. There is always a margin of self-definition. Rather than determinism there are the irrepressible Bellovian asserters (Augie, Henderson, Herzog, Bummidge). But Freud introduces a determinism deeper than any Augie could imagine, the determinism of the unconscious mind. "What a man thinks he is doing counts for nothing," writes Bellow in a draft of Herzog. "All his work in the world is done by impulses he will never understand—sinful to the priest, sexual to the psychiatrist." Freud said that character was essentially fixed by the age of six, that everything in character was essentially determined by that time. "In most cases," as Philip Rieff says, "Freud insists that character does not change deliberately, through taking thought or through decision; our character is, so to speak, changed for us, by returns from oblivion" (*Freud: The Mind of the Moralist*). This applies to genius as well. So when a Leonardo abandons art for science, it is because his infantile past has gained control over him. The biblical Moses may be considered an heroic exception of conscious self-determination in Freud, and this is a reason why *Moses and Monotheism* has not been influential with the orthodox Freudians. Needless to say, the discovery that childhood experiences are of the greatest importance and that their effects are unconscious is momentous. Yet Freud's emphasis on these truths almost precludes autonomy. Thus the Freudian revisionists withdraw from his determinism. "Freud did not envision people in terms of developing powers and as total personalities," says Clara Thompson. "He thought of them much more mechanistically—as victims of the search for the release of tension" (*Psychoanalysis: Evolution and Development*). In their critique of determinism and victimization, the revisionists are expressing a humanist concern, one similar to Bellow's, and they do so with an ambivalence not unlike his. For the revisionists, Freud often mistakes cultural phenomena for instinctual ones. Bellow, as we shall see, does not regard the matter with such anthropological detachment, which substitutes a cultural for a biological determinism. But for him, as for the revisionists, the root of the problem is the nature of the Freudian unconscious.

By *unconscious* Bellow means the place first indicated by Freud in the final chapter of *The Interpretation of Dreams* and made more emphatic in *The Ego and the Id* and *New Introductory Lectures;* in other words, the dynamic unconscious which implies a function, not merely the descriptive which implies a quality. If it is a place, it is not an especially pleasant one. "The desire to murder is actually present in the unconscious," says Freud (*Totem and Taboo*). The Bellow protagonist is not unfamiliar with that desire. A central theme in Bellow is the overcoming of that impulse, an impulse which is for him indicative of nihilism. In *Totem and Taboo,* murder (the Oedipal killing of the father, the primal crime) does take place, followed by a complex reaction expressing the primal ambivalence and thereby the beginnings of civilization. Professor Herzog addresses himself to just this issue as he waits in his dreary cell after his traffic accident: *"If a primal crime is the origin of social order, as Freud, Roheim et cetera believe, the bond of brothers attacking and murdering the primal father, eating his body, gaining their freedom by a murder and united by a blood wrong, then there is some reason why jail should have these dark tones."* But the perception is fleeting: *"All that is nothing but metaphor. I can't truly feel I can attribute my blundering to this thick unconscious cloud. This primitive blood-daze."* Indeed, his actions, superior to violence and murder, suggest that he should not. This is why he writes in "cheerful eagerness." Herzog sees something other than murderous egotism in the deepest recesses of the unconscious, something which refuses to disappear. *"The dream of man's heart, however much we may distrust and resent it, is that life may complete itself in significant pattern."* Freud may agree with this in the last analysis, but not in the first, and therein lies a great difference. The congenital optimist, Herzog knows that *"you got one last chance to know justice. Truth."* Characteristically, he puts things in traditional, moralistic terms. He does not deny the existence of an unconscious, only its Freudian character.

Bellow has said, "the unconscious is anything that human beings don't know. Is there any reason why we have to accept Freud's account of what it is that we don't know? . . . Is it possible that what we don't know has a metaphysical character and not a Freudian, naturalistic character? I think that the unconscious is a concept that begs the question and simply returns us to our ignorance with an arrogant attitude of confidence, and that is why I am against it." Bellow is not giving us a positivist unconscious. In this view the unconscious is that of which we are *ex hypothesi* unaware; therefore nothing can be said about it; it is, then, effectively nonexistent. Bellow's metaphysical unconscious is taken on what Santayana calls animal faith. This faith assumes a First Cause which may be called God. Rieff rightly calls Freud's unconscious a "god-term" (Kenneth Burke's words) or "Freud's conceptual ultimate, a First Cause, to be believed in precisely because it is both fundamental to and inaccessible to experience." In effect, Freud attempts "to eliminate religious experience by paralleling it" (Philip Rieff, "Introduction" to D. H. Lawrence, *Psychoanalysis and the Unconscious, Fantasia of the Unconscious*).

Bellow reverses the primary burden of the unknown, choosing to make upward rather than downward comparisons, outward, not just inward comparisons. He wants feeling without symbols, where Freud could not do without symbols. Dreams are, for Freud, the language of determinism, the truth of a totally symbolic, amoral chaos of an unconscious. Freud saw the drama of sleep but not so clearly the drama of being awake. If, as Rieff suggests, free association proves that we are never free, the primacy of dream symbolism implies a stereotyped psychological incarceration, a permanent state of house arrest. Kafka is the great novelist of this mood. Bellow suspects that symbolic interpretation may be an abrogation of free will, a way the unconscious can tyrannize over consciousness, the obscure motive over spontaneity. The result can be a scholasticism which infects not only the Freudian world but the literary world as well. "Deep readers of the world beware," Bellow once warned. "You may never again see common daylight." Freud tells us that though the ego appears autonomous and unitary, marked off distinctly from anything else, it really is "continued inward, without any sharp delimitation into an unconscious mental entity which we designate as the id and for which it serves as a facade." The downward and the inward movement is honorific in Freud, the true source, but the upward and outward is on a tight leash of sublimation. The metaphysical, the religious—these are, for Freud, ways of wrapping the self in a batting of excelsior.

Herzog's resistance to the Freudian unconscious issues into an engaging insight. In a letter to Spinoza, he agrees with the philosopher that thoughts not causally connected may cause pain. *"It may interest you to know,"* he writes, *"that in the twentieth century random association is believed to yield up the deepest secrets of the psyche."* While free association may be the ultimate insult to rational purposiveness, the process itself can yield some of the mysteries of the deep. One can argue that Spinoza overvalued reason; in any case, Freud surely knew something that Spinoza did not.

Whether, or to what extent, the unconscious is Freudian, it is certainly there. Free association, like the psychopathology of everyday life, is, much more than chaos, a triumph over it. Herzog knows the rules but does not want to play the game, *"believing that reason can make steady progress from disorder to harmony and that the conquest of chaos need not be begun anew every day."* But isn't there such "progress" in psychoanalysis? Herzog is saved from smugness here by the precariousness of his claim: "How I wish it! How I wish it were so! How Moses prayed for this." The yearning for moral clarity even more than the clarity itself is the characteristic Herzog note. His prayer for reason is humanism in the defensive position.

A draft of Herzog's letter to Spinoza undermines the foundation of Freud's unconscious by dismissing its current neo-Freudian expression. Freud holds that "what decides the purpose of life is simply the programme of the pleasure principle. This principle dominates the operation of the mental apparatus from the start." Rather than happiness, however, this brings unhappiness through an elaborate sequence of repression and renunciation. "One feels inclined to say that the intention that men should be 'happy' is not included in the plan of 'Creation,' " says Freud. Adhering to a different view of the pleasure principle, the neo-Freudians have given us Freud without pain. Bellow rejects the biological determinism of both by denying the cardinality of pleasure. That he has to complain to Spinoza may be ominous. But is there anyone better around to talk to? Herzog writes, *"I subscribed at one time to the theory that it was pleasure and pleasure only that gave one the strength to be moral, that pleasure was fundamentally a question of health, and that the only possible source of goodness and happiness was instinctual gratification. I no longer believe this to be true."* He communicates with Spinoza as he and Ramona embrace. She bites his lip in ecstasy. *"This theory did me a lot of harm,"* he continues. The comedy of contemporary life does not keep his moralism down: "I think that John Stuart Mill was absolutely right: happiness cannot be a direct object. Must be a by-product." Marriage to Ramona would be an ideological misalliance. Not the pleasure principle but self-directed purpose ought to determine. Something close to this opposition was made some time ago by Aristotle, who distinguished between pleasure as sensation and pleasure as activity. The latter in Bellow's humanistic view has more to do with happiness.

Freud's conception of the eternal recurrence of the Oedipal drama reduces religion to psychology and history to nature. History becomes a sort of secular predestination, with the unconscious as a weedy Garden of Eden, the primal crime as Original Sin. For Bellow, Freud minimizes and perhaps destroys pure motive in a way that victimizes the Christian as well as the natural man. *"Charity,"* Herzog writes to Edvig, *"as if it didn't have enough trouble in this day and age, will always be suspected of morbidity—sado-masochism, perversity of some sort. All higher or moral tendencies lie under suspicion of being rackets."* Herzog is angry at Edvig's indifference to his attempted *agape* in dealing with Mady, an indifference which destroys an aspect of the Judeo-Christian tradition he believes is real. *"If my soul, out of Season, out of place, experienced these higher emotions, I could get no credit for them anyway. Not from you with your attitude toward good intentions. I've read your stuff about the psychological realism of Calvin. I hope you don't mind my saying that it reveals a lousy, cringing, grudging conception of human nature. This is how I see your Protestant Freudianism."*

The friction between humanism and the Freudian unconscious surfaces again in Freud's view of history. Since history is nature and the unconscious determines, pre-history is more important than history in the conventional sense. Though psychoanalysis is an historical process for the individual patient, it also aims to uncover the individual equivalent of pre-history. Accordingly, Freud's writings on culture are more concerned with myth than history. "For the very reason that Hegel thought Africa no proper subject for the historian, Freud thought it most proper," Rieff says. Bellow's Africa, on the other hand, is really an affirmation of traditional morality. And in much of his work Bellow is involved with historical reality as such. His time is chronological, not mythological. The momentous event has not occurred in an archetypal past but is unfolding before our contemporaneous eyes. We know what the momentous event is for Freud.

Anyone reading Freud with a clear eye will see that the Oedipus complex cannot be explained away in mollifying cultural terms. Freud really means it. However tentative and delicate his rhetorical poses, he never comes up with anything more suited to his purpose, and suggestion soon becomes fact. He sees nothing in history to cause him to change his mind. *"Homo homini lupus,"* says Freud in *Civilization and Its Discontents* (a sentiment uttered in manuscript by Bellow's Winkelman of *The Last Analysis* as he thinks about contemporary reality in Balzacian terms). "Who in the face of all his experience of life and of history, will have the courage to dispute this assertion." Bellow longs to accord to human nature the value that Freud grants to civilization. Renunciation is Freud's heroism. Bellow sees its importance, but he resents the parsimony implied by its prevalence in the Freudian system.

II

Comparing Bellow and Freud as thinkers points up perhaps more clearly than anything else can the religious tendency of Bellow's humanism. Bellow's hostility to Freud may be seen as the obverse of Freud's hostility to the religious temperament. He explicitly attacks Freud's "A Religious Experience" for displaying systematic rigidity comparable to that of Marx: "Once you've given yourself over to one of these systems, you've lost your freedom in a very significant degree." Here then is Freudianism-as-ideology criticized from the point of view of humanist independence. Bellow recognizes that Freud was "a great genius" and recalls what "my feelings were quite early in life when I began to read Freud. It was hard not to see the world in terms of instinct and repression, not to see it in terms of concavity and convexity, not to see it in terms of the struggle of the child with his parents, and so on." Ever the writer, he sees these as "metaphors," as he sees all philosophy from the point of view of imagination. The individual must be moved, and Freud has moved him. "A Religious Experience" has crystallized his contempt. An American doctor had read *The Future of an Illusion* and writes to Freud saying, "I too at one time lost my faith" when as a medical student the body of a "very beautiful old woman" was brought into the dissecting room. He "could no longer believe in a god" who would do such a thing. But the doctor thinks about it and recovers his faith, recommending that Freud too "postpone a final decision on the existence of God for a time." Bellow is outraged by Freud's response, which equates the cadaver with the doctor's mother. "At this moment," he says, "I experienced a violent reaction against Freud. Was it not possible to experience beauty or pity without thinking of your mother, or without the Oedipus complex? The rigidity of this repels me. I felt that it was coarse and cruel. It's this sort of thing that I think of when I think of Freud."

There is more to Freud's piece than Bellow's recollection of it, and what is left out, to be analytic about it, may be as much the reason for Bellow's having selected this minor essay from among many more obvious illustrations. The piece is more explicitly Oedipal than Bellow seems to remember. "Why was it," Freud asks, "that his indignation against God broke out precisely when he received this particular impression in the dissecting room?" Freud equates "his desire to destroy his father" with "doubt in the existence of God." Bellow speaks of the purity of human motive, but, given his own preferences, he might almost as well have spoken of the purity of belief. Freud concludes with just the sort of certitude that repels him: "The new impulse, which was displaced into the sphere of religion, was only a repetition of the Oedipal situation and consequently soon met with a similar fate. It succumbed to a powerful opposing current. . . . The conflict seems to have been unfolded in the form of hallucinatory psychosis: inner voices were heard which uttered warnings against resistance to God. . . . The outcome . . . was a kind predetermined by the fate of the Oedipus complex: complete submission to the will of God the Father." Lying supine is a posture which invites the devil, warns the beleaguered Monsignor Sheen in his book on psychoanalysis. Freud's explanation rivals that of his sometime explanation of love remembered by Herzog as "a psychosis, usually brief." Is belief psychosis? Bellow thinks not. Yet it is significant that the humanistic rather than the religious content of the piece most sharply elicits Bellow's ire.

"Is it not true," asks Freud in *The Future of an Illusion*, "that the two main points in the modern educational programme are the retardation of sexual development and the early application of religious influence?" Freud laments this Victorian asymmetry and wonders how people "dominated by thought prohibitions" will "attain the psychological ideal, the primacy of the intelligence." But what if the situation is reversed? What if the spiritual is more repressed than the sexual? The id triumphant and the superego underground? Body open and soul furtive? This may be said to have been the situation in America at least from the mid-sixties through the seventies. The consequences for psychoanalysis were great. A Freudian analyst speaks of this topsy-turvy swing of history. Virginity was once a value, notes Henry Lowenfeld; now perhaps it is a taboo ("Psychoanalysis Today," *Partisan Review* 48 [1981]). He cites the case of a patient who broke her hymen with a shampoo bottle. As for the psychoanalytic ethic of honesty, there is the young woman who invites her four-year-old son to watch her sexual performance with different lovers. Lowenfeld believes that children do not introject parents anymore but parents introject children. The decline of the superego is the root of the problem, signifying the weakened role of the father and the eclipse of religion. The Oedipus complex is not resolved. Rather than hysteria or obsessional neurosis, the neurotic constellations of sexual liberation are depression, emptiness, inability to love. There is a problem for libido theory. You can cure frigidity but what can you do for promiscuity? Much of Bellow's writing since *Herzog*—the sexual grotesquerie might almost have come out of *Mr. Sammler's Planet*—responds to this second reversed reality.

To speak of religion in Bellow, then, is to speak of it in a cultural predicament quite different from Freud's. Freud was slaying a dragon; Bellow is preserving a dinosaur. Though he has little sympathy for ritual orthodoxy, he has far less for Freud's description of religion as universal obsessional neurosis. Herzog rejects just this term. For Bellow, as for the religious man, superego is not primarily equated with a usually repressive society, not part of the Oedipal drama writ large. Aware of "the harm done by people of high principles," Herzog nonetheless records his dissent from the psychoanalytic view: "Instead of laying the blame as Freud does on the excess of superego, I would say that the doing of good relieves the poor burdened human soul." For Bellow, conscience remains intact as a means of individual assertion, in an age where many have confused it with pleasure. Like the believer, Bellow thinks that psychoanalysis undermines morality. Freud advocates nothing. D. H. Lawrence was right in saying that this is why he can never "get down to the rock on which he must build his church." Rieff puts it precisely in saying that Lawrence charges Freud with having "forgotten the prayerful attitude that man ought to have toward himself." Bellow's Gonzaga puts the contemporary lack of moral intensity more dramatically: *"Go away. You have no holy ones"* (*Seize the Day*). Though certainly not in Lawrentian terms, it is fair to say that Bellow desires to express the prayerful attitude. Augie March's sense of the *amor futi* as blessedness rather than indifference, Tommy Wilhelm's funeral parlor transfiguration, Henderson's self-proclaimed "mediumistic and attuned" soul, Herzog's addressing God as "Thou," Sammler's knowledge of the contract, Citrine's musing on Humboldt's transcendence—all of these attest to the prayerful attitude.

What, then, is the quality of Bellow's belief? Erich Fromm's distinction between authoritarian and humanistic religion takes us close to the answer. The first involves self-abasement, subjection of the individual to a higher end, the "fear and trembling" of contrition. The powers of the self are projected onto God. The soul or self is slight compared to life after death or the Fatherland. Humanistic religion, on the other hand, is "centered around man and his strength." It does, of course, imply a oneness with the "All," and it is "theistic"; however, it insists that "God is a symbol of *man's powers*" (*Psychoanalysis and Religion*). Spinoza is an example. He affirmed God's immanence but denied his transcendence (for which, we may note, he was excommunicated). In the humanist perspective, as Fromm sees it, the teachings of Buddha, Isaiah, Christ, Socrates and Spinoza are the same. In humanistic religion, "conscience is not the internalized voice of authority but man's own voice, the guardian of our integrity. . . . Sin is not primarily sin against God but sin against ourselves." Obedience is not the issue.

As a Jew out of the synagogue, a man who defines religious feeling largely in reaction to a profound lack in the secular life in which he is saturated, Bellow is certainly distant from authoritarian religion. Some may think that he is distant from religion altogether, lacking in the commitment (which may necessarily include institutional involvement) that makes it a way of life. Be that as it may, Bellow is more attuned to tradition than Fromm's distinctions will allow. For Bellow, God is not merely a symbol of man's powers or a symbol of anything. God is not simply immanent but transcendent and, usually, the Jewish God. He is "Thou" but he is not, as Herzog puts it in manuscript, "God the Father, above the clouds. I don't believe in that." Conscience is man's own voice but a voice with a transcendental yearning.

The ending of *Herzog* is perhaps the clearest case in point. Herzog is not without some self-abasement (*"My face too blind, my mind too limited, my instincts too narrow"*), but God, somehow personal, is defined in terms of Herzog's emotional response to Him (*"Thou movest me"*). There is always the humanistic questioning (*"But this intensity, doesn't it mean anything? Is it an idiot joy that makes this animal, the most peculiar animal of all, exclaim something?"*). Yet reason will take him only so far (*"But I have no arguments to make about it"*). Just as his faith receives support from Nature (*"Something produces intensity, a holy feeling, as oranges produce orange, as grass green, as birds heat"*), his God concludes in man (*"I am pretty well satisfied to be, to be just as it is willed, and for as long as I may remain in occupancy"*).

If Fromm's sense of the unity of spiritual worthies is rather indiscriminate, we may recall that Sammler's fascination with Eckhart and Citrine's with Rudolf Steiner is no less universalizing. Bellow's is not the belief of perfect faith. Faith may even surprise the Bellow protagonist, issuing usually from an unshakable sense of the ethical. "I wilfully misread my contract," thinks Herzog in a characteristic metaphor of obligation. "I never was the principal, but only on loan to myself," he continues, using a metaphor that Hattie Waggoner of "Leaving the Yellow House" also uses. She is on loan from her real, that is, unconscious self, the reservoir of her spirit. Herzog, however, is on loan from above rather than below: "Evidently I continue to believe in God. Though never admitting it. But what else explains my conduct and my life?" His subsequent recoil from murder is to make that explanation even more clear. Having reached a plateau of moral clarity, Herzog earns the right to correspond with God—a humanist assumption! The man of letters in the religious world. His words to God are very much those of humanist religion. *"How my mind has struggled to make coherent sense,"* says our seeker of the morally real. Contemporaneous as his words are, they have a trace of humility: *"I have not been too good at it. But have desired to do your unknowable will, taking it, and you, without symbols. Everything of intensest significance."* God is emotionally charged meaning, value, an immediate experience, an authentic illumination not to be diluted by constructs standing for something else (e.g., Freudian symbolism). This is not authoritarian religion but the humanist religion that equates God with the highest, purest feeling. He adds, with the post-Romantic, postmodern psychological fatigue not to be confused with religious self-abasement: *"Especially if divested of me."* Herzog's salvation is freedom from the cult of sensibility. In a draft of a letter to Monsignor Hilton, Herzog writes: *"If I had to put it in my own way,"* and he always does, *"I would say that to be inescapably closed up in a world of one's own making is hell."* Herzog knows the condition first-hand, and he calls the transcendence of it God.

"Love thy neighbor as thyself"—Fromm says that this is the essence of religion. But he didn't count on an era of self-hatred. There seems to be nothing in the humorless analyst that would put him in touch with our wrenching comedy on this subject. Herzog does pay more than lip-service to "our employment by other human beings and their employment by us" as the "real and essential question," but he does not have the answer. Nor do any of the later Bellow protagonists, much as they may want it. Cain and Abel, rather than Oedipus, are central to the Judeo-Christian tradition. The issue of responsibility for the other person has always been a difficult one. "Am I my brother's keeper?" is, in its original context, a rhetorical question raised by a maniac. All the more reason that the answer must be yes. If the mutual love of brothers is difficult, how much more difficult is that of neighbors. In *Civilization and Its Discontents,* Freud says the Golden Rule is "impossible to fulfill." Bellow would have to agree that "such an enormous inflation of love can only lower its value," but he would reject Freud's contention that it is "a commandment which is really justified by the fact that nothing else runs so strongly counter to the original nature of man." While not so optimistic as Fromm, he is not so pessimistic as Freud.

Freud has contempt for what Fromm defines as humanist religion, the poetized religion of "as if," God as symbol in a universe of tolerant cultural relativism. The pious neurotics at least had belief, not just spiritual need. On this point it is important to emphasize that Fromm's humanism excludes actual belief but Bellow's does not. Bellow easily meets Fromm's criteria for the religious mentality: (1) wonder (2) "ultimate concern" (Tillich) (3) oneness of separate self with All. The first two the Bellow protagonist typically exhibits, the last less fully, though Bellow dramatizes it shamelessly, if wryly, in *Humboldt's Gift*. Freud would have said that Citrine can't let go of poppa and thus exhibits the infantilism of the oceanic feeling. As for "ultimate concern," Freud writes to Marie Bonaparte that, "The moment a man questions the meaning and value of life he is sick, since objectively neither has any existence." Man may seek the light but it will only give him another insight into darkness. On this assumption, wonder cannot be pristine but only an experience of darkness overcome. Bellow would counter that these are prime illustrations of the usual psychoanalytic reductiveness. "You're a hard-nosed man," shouts Bummidge to his "analyst." "Why do you prefer the ugliest interpretations? Why do you pollute all my good impulses?" (*LA*).

Freud does acknowledge the civilizing tendencies of religion, even in its most primitive form. In *Totem and Taboo* he writes, "It is difficult to resist the notion that, long before a table of laws was handed down by any god, these savages were in possession of a living commandment: 'Thou shalt not kill,' a violation of which would not go unpunished." Freud sees religion as the origin of ethics. Curiously, Freud comes back every now and then to the one religious (cultural) commandment that most fascinates Bellow, one that provides a stay against nihilistic chaos. Even a tyrant or a dictator, says Freud in *The Future of An Illusion,* "has every reason to want others to keep at least one cultural commandment: thou shalt not kill." The alternative for Freud is intolerable. "How short-sighted," he says, "to strive for the abolition of culture! What would then remain would be the state of nature, and that is far harder to endure." The state of nature for Bellow is not so nearly Hobbesian, though in *Mr. Sammler's Planet* and, particularly, in *The Dean's December,* it almost is. In any case, the prohibition against murder does not amount to religion.

There is an important distinction to be drawn in the ways Bellow and Freud view the act of murder. Freud sees all murder as part of the Oedipal drama, thereby shedding a brilliant light on, say, the Oedipal Dostoevsky. In his essay "Dostoevsky and Parricide," Freud considers *The Brothers Karamazov, Oedipus Rex* and *Hamlet* as Oedipal dramas which, being three of the greatest works of literature, lend indirect support to his interpretation of psychological experience. Of the murder in Dostoevsky's novel Freud writes, "It is a matter of indifference who committed the crime; psychology is interested only in discovering who desired it, and who welcomed it when it was done, and for that reason, all the brothers are equally guilty." Because of the Oedipal reality in Dostoevsky, "the criminal is to him almost a Redeemer, who has taken on himself the guilt which others would otherwise have had to bear. One need not now commit murder, after he has committed murder, but one must be grateful to him, because without him, one would oneself have to have been a murderer." This interpretation can be documented in *The Brothers Karamazov*, which gives us a father well worth killing. But Freud makes virtually the same point in his discussion of tragedy in *Totem and Taboo*, where he speaks of the tragic hero in general. The primal crime underlies all: "In the remote reality it had actually been the members of the Chorus who caused the Hero's suffering; now, however, they exhausted themselves with sympathy and regret, and it was the Hero himself who was responsible for his own sufferings. The crime which was thrown on to his shoulders, presumptuousness and rebelliousness against a great authority, was precisely the crime for which the members of the Chorus, the company of brothers, was responsible. Thus the tragic Hero becomes, though it might be against his will, the redeemer of the Chorus." Here as elsewhere, the brilliance of Freud's perceptions makes one feel that, anthropological evidence to the contrary notwithstanding, there must be a rightness to what he says.

Yet a crucial moral distinction remains. For Bellow, and for humanism generally, there is all the difference in the world between committing a murder and wishing to do so, between impulse and deed. Bellow has said that this is a distinction between the Jewish and Christian points of view: "The Jewish outlook is that unless you have actually committed the crime you are not guilty of it, no matter what you have thought or dreamed." This is also the humanist and liberal view. Man may be vulnerable, the capacity for evil (*yetzer ha-ra* in the old Hebrew expression) may be always present, but so is the capacity for good, and in the struggle between them lies the reality of moral life. For Freud and for a certain kind of Christianity, determinism or predestination essentially obliterated the distinction between wish and act. Nowhere are Bellow's humanist sympathies vis-à-vis Freudianism more clearly drawn in terms of moral emphasis. The assertions of free will in Bellow may be small but there is, for example, a crucial difference between Herzog's desire to murder and his decision not to. It is the criminal who is guilty, but we are not "equally guilty" (as Freud puts it). The problem is complex, for as Freud says in "Dostoevsky and Parricide": "A moral man is one who reacts to the temptation he feels in his heart without yielding to it." In other words, Freud does make a distinction between what psychology is "interested in" and what morality is "interested in." Psychology is not ethics; health values are not moral values. Granted. But any system has moral implications and there is a key difference here: in Bellow there is the attraction of the good, in Freud the renunciation of the bad. As Rieff puts it: "Freud could not speak of the desire to be good in the same sense that he could speak of desiring what we have to renounce for the good. Surely this is one-sided. Aspiration may be as genuine as desire, and as original." With his emphasis on the sway of the unconscious, Freud is nothing if not profound. But there can be the greatest depth in the obvious. Freud sees this when he considers biological desire (e.g., the babe at its mother's breast) but does not when he weighs moral desire. His dark view of human nature misses the profundity of simplicity. If the good can ever be considered simple.

Yet Bellow and Freud share a skepticism about the extremity of Dostoevskian goodness, that "rage for goodness so near to vileness and murderousness," as Albert Corde puts it (*The Dean's December,* [all further references to this text will be abbreviated as *DD*]). Neither is satisfied with the "murder-saviour" type, which Corde sees in the relatively moderate Toby Winthrop, and both see in Raskolnikov and Stavrogin. "It was foreign, bookish—it was Dostoevsky stuff that the vices of Sodom coexisted with the adoration of Holy Sophia," says Corde (*DD*). Bellow characterizes this as abstract modern consciousness, but Freud has a clearer explanation of the phenomenon in its acute Dostoevskian manifestation. He is skeptical of penitence which "becomes a technique to enable murder to be done." In *The Future of an Illusion* he states the social raison d'être for "the sublime conclusion" of Russian mysticism "that sin is indispensable for the full enjoyment of the blessing of divine grace, and therefore fundamentally . . . pleasing to God." Freud says, "It is well known that the priests could only keep the masses submissive to religion by making these great concessions to human instincts." Freud attacks the holy sinner as part of his argument to undermine religion, which he sees as authoritarian. Bellow, in his humanist stance, never without some skepticism about religion even in Sammler and Citrine, has Corde say, "So what was this pure-in-spirit bit? For an American who had been around, a man in his mid-fifties, this beatitude language was unreal" (*DD*). Religion must meet the humanist requirement of reason.

III

Despite this point of similarity, Freud's essay on "Dostoevsky and Parricide" illustrates still another sharp difference between Bellow and Freud, their relationship to art, literature in particular. Brilliant as it is,

Freud's piece treats Dostoevsky more as a case than a writer. Freud finds Dostoevsky fascinating for the clarity with which he confirms the Oedipal drama. Freud's interest in content, then, is of a special kind. He has no interest in formal or stylistic matters and not even much interest in thematic ones. *The Brothers Karamazov* is mainly an instance of Dostoevsky's personality, particularly his neurotic configurations and how they damaged his artistic mission. The illumination of a psychoanalytically relevant pattern takes the place of moral and aesthetic evaluation of a work, which is why Freud may make much of a work that has little literary significance (e.g., Jensen's *Gradiva*). Freud gives us dazzling insights into Dostoevsky the neurotic, but he cannot really tell us why his work is good or bad, great or mediocre. In these ways, Freud's treatment of Dostoevsky is similar to his treatment of Leonardo.

Freud is, in fact, uneasy with art. Otto Rank maintained that Freudian theory could not cope with the creative artist. And Freud seems to agree with him. It is in the essay on "Dostoevsky and Parricide" that Freud issued this famous disclaimer: "Unfortunately, before the problem of the creative artist, analysis must lay down its arms." Why is this so? Because there is something about art that eludes the theory of unconscious determinism, there is something that is larger than Freud's system. This has for a long time been Bellow's opinion. And art is not, in his view, the only thing that is larger than Freud's system. As Herzog puts it (in manuscript), referring to just this remark, "Freud confessed he laid down his arms before the problem of art. He should have surrendered to all the mysteries of high inspiration, including the work of moral genius." Again Bellow insists that there is an area of freedom that Freudian rationalism does not comprehend.

Lionel Trilling has written of the similarities between literature and psychoanalysis, which is "a science of tropes, of metaphor and its variants, synecdoche and metonymy (*The Liberal Imagination*). And everyone knows Freud's claim that it was not he but the poets who discovered the unconscious. But what unconscious was it that "they" discovered? Not one that defines art as daydream, escape from reality, mild narcosis, or "substitute gratification" for "the oldest cultural renunciations." Freud thinks it unfortunate that psychoanalysis must throw up its hands before "the problem" of art, but it is fortunate from the artist's point of view. Art is freedom of expression, health rather than sickness, genius rather than neurosis. Freud never grants to art the autonomy the artist gives it. He sees the imagination as a symptom of the unconscious. In this sense he values criticism over art. The interpretation of the subject is the key to art just as psychoanalysis is the key to the unconscious. As a novelist who values imagination, as a humanist whose art takes a particularly moral turn, as a human being who believes in the primacy of inspiration. Bellow could not agree with these formulations. "If I hold with Freud in anything," says Bellow, "I would hold with him in this one matter, that reality is a projection of something or other. Fictions are fascinating and relatively coherent projections." He sees the novel, however, as a projection of "truth, or of reality," terms which do not correspond to Freud's idea of religion as a projection of revolt against the father or art as a projection of unconscious wish-fulfillment. To the term "truth" Freud prefers "fantasy."

Bellow's criticism of Freud does not break new ground as such. Rather it is a profound version of the familiar criticism Freud termed "unjust" in *The Ego and the Id,* when he said that "psycho-analysis has been reproached time after time with ignoring the higher, moral, supra-personal side of human nature." Freud claims that his critics ignore the nature of the ego and superego, "the representative of our relation to our parents." But his ego-ideal or superego remains an outgrowth of Oedipal struggle. That is, Freud's moral world follows his limiting terminology, and it is a world which becomes increasingly claustral. Bellow is in essential agreement with Rieff's view of Freud as a modern thinker, as one who gives us a weak ego and an oppressive superego, with the nihilistic problematics this entails.

But Bellow is in radical disagreement with Rieff as to the consequences of seeing Freud this way. In Rieff's books on Freud and psychoanalytic theory, the author accepts with open arms the diminished concept of the self which it has been Bellow's task to repudiate. Where the protagonist of a Bellow work is typically a citizen-hero, Rieff speaks of a "citizen-patient." Although Rieff is wary of seeing "an admittedly sick society in terms of that subtlest . . . authoritarian image, the hospital," this is exactly what he does. If one can speak of a sociologist of mind having a controlling metaphor, this is Rieff's: "In the emergent democracy of the sick . . . [the] hospital is succeeding the church and the parliament as the archetypal institution of Western culture." Freud is "the first out-patient of the hospital culture in which we live." In *The Triumph of the Therapeutic,* Rieff predicts that "modern society will mount psychodramas far more frequently than its ancestors mounted miracle plays, with patient-analysts acting out their inner lives, after which they could extemporize the final act as interpretation." Rieff calls this "hospital-theater." What Rieff considers serious, Bellow considers farce in *The Last Analysis.* The fruits of hospital culture may be strange. "We are, I fear, getting to know one another," says Rieff. With his combination of elegance and lugubriousness, good will and fatalism, Rieff at times reminds one of no one as much as the old radio character Digby Odell, "your friendly undertaker," who nowadays would be reincarnated as your genial therapist. Freud saw ethics as a "therapeutic" activity of the superego, assuming by this metaphor the sick person as the norm. Making the same assumption, Rieff sees any "system or moralizing demands" as "therapy," the "therapeutic" goal being "a manipulatable sense of well-being."

It is precisely this view that Charlie Citrine attacks in *Humboldt's Gift* when Cantabile, looking through his library, asks about *The Triumph of the Therapeutic* (a phrase which first appears in Selma Fraiberg's negative review of Rieff's book on Freud). Citrine is quite clear about his dislike of the book: "It says that psychotherapists may become the new spiritual leaders of mankind. A disaster. Goethe was afraid the modern world might turn into a hospital. Every citizen unwell." Rieff sees this new psychological man benignly as "the healthy hypochondriac." But Citrine can only wonder whether "hypochondria" is "a creation of the medical profession," concluding with a flourish: "According to this author, when culture fails to deal with the feeling of emptiness and the panic to which man is disposed (and he does say 'disposed') other agents come forward to put us together with therapy, with glue, or slogans, or spit, or as that fellow Gumbein [Harold Rosenberg] the art critic says, poor wretches are recycled on the couch. This view is even more pessimistic than the one held by Dostoevsky's Grand Inquisitor. . . . A natural disposition to feelings of emptiness and panic is worse than that. Much worse. What it really means is that we human beings are insane. The last institution which controlled such insanity (on this view) was the Church" (*Humboldt's Gift*, [all further references to this text will be abbreviated as *HG*]). Rieff inverts Pangloss so as to say that the therapeutic is the best of all possible worlds.

It is true, as Rieff claims, that "the understanding of normal character through the neurotic character, of health through sickness, is Freud's master trope." This method surely is at the heart of Freud's genius, but it may, finally, give us a greater insight into sickness than health. Moreover, it may impose a modernist norm where none exists. The matter of Freud's master trope could be put quite differently. "Freud could build a theory of human nature," says Irving Kristol, "on the basis of his experience with hysterics and neurotics, a unique and strange achievement which testifies to our modern psychic equilibrium, whose fulcrum is at the edge of an abyss" ("God and the Psychoanalysts," *Commentary* [1949]). A skeptical humanist balance resides in this perspective, with which Bellow would be sympathetic. Rieff acknowledges that "there is a fatal lack of commitment

about Freud's ideal type. To be busy, spirited, and self-confident is a goal
that will inspire only those who have resigned the ghosts of older and no-
bler aspirations." Yet Rieff willingly does so. Unlike Freud, Bellow constructs a past that he can honor, and he is in frequent, perhaps too
frequent, correspondence with its ghosts.

IV

Though Bellow rejects Freudian thought in these fundamental respects, he is nonetheless sympathetic to and sometimes indebted to it in
others. An admirer of Montaigne, an observer of local mores, Bellow is,
like Freud, very well aware of the cost of the civilization he defends. A
character like Artur Sammler knows a good deal about renunciation. Yet
Freud's attributing all civilization to renunciation seems to Bellow unnec-
essarily severe. "Take what you want," says the Spanish proverb, "and
pay for it." Freud is the genius of this theme, one which Bellow fully understands. No one is so taken up with psychic costs as Freud, our econo-
mist of the self. Indeed, he knows as well the cost of many things you
never even get to "take." But it may be that life has its unexpected re-
wards, its serendipitous moments, its joys unmixed with pain. Or at least
if not that a possibility of accomplishment for which one need not go half-
way to castration. It may be that, with Augie March, one can perceive the
blessedness in the *amor fati*. Or that, with Herzog, one can be moved by
the principle of creation.

To the extent that Freudian disillusion is a repudiation of utopian pro-
gressivism, Bellow endorses it. Both reject Marx, knowing the essentialist
wisdom of *plus ça change plus c'est la même chose* (though Herzog feels or
hopes that there are good human qualities yet to be discovered). They are
both conservative liberals (if Freud can be called liberal in any sense) who
place personality above politics, knowing, stoically, that the self must be
defined in the face of constant crisis. Both recognize the need to recover
instinct. Though Bellow thinks Freud inflates the pleasure principle, both
abide by some version of the reality principle, preferring reason to primal
energy. Yet Bellow gives much more to intuition and inspiration, is more
trusting of emotional response. *"Trouve avant de chercher,"* says Charlie
Citrine (quoting Valéry). "This finding before seeking was my special gift.
If I had any" (*HG*). Citrine's is the very reverse of the Freudian procedure.
Given the Freudian system, the chances are that one will find what one is
looking for, and what one finds will not be very nice. "We may reject the
existence of an original, as it were natural, capacity to distinguish good

from bad," says Freud. Bellow is not so disillusioned, holding with Sammler that "we know." With his metaphors of contract and obligation, Bellow is more Jewish. Jokes and family feeling, integrity and argumentativeness may not a Jew make. Though these are more indicative than pinochle and cabanas, or sleeping on Saturday afternoon, Freud's Jewish identity remains much more problematic than Bellow's. But they both have one. As if in tacit homage, most of the Bellow protagonists have read Freud—even, in one manuscript, Eugene Henderson. And there is frequent reference in Bellow to psychoanalytic terminology. There may even be a rare instance of an image Bellow has taken over from Freud in his fiction, consciously or unconsciously.

As a novelist who pursues self-definition partly through a recapturing of childhood experience, Bellow's occupation parallels Freud's. Both Freud and Herzog have their "personal histories, old tales from old times that may not be worth remembering." Both literature and psychoanalysis posit the primacy of emotion. To complement Bellow's humanism, Freud is more of a thinker than a scientist. He thought of himself as a humanist rather than a physician. Some Bellow characters, perhaps too many, read like case histories—Tommy Wilhelm and Dr. Adler being the most prominent—but Henderson, Herzog, Mady and Humboldt may be so considered. Herzog does not seem to mind, thinking jauntily, "If I am out of my mind, it's all right with me." He is diagnosed as a reactive-depressive. A certain psychological disarray is essential to Bellow's comic sense. More than this, there are times when we seem to be eavesdropping on an analytic session, as in the following reflection from *Herzog:* "What I seem to do, thought Herzog, is to inflame myself voluptuously, esthetically, until I reach a sexual climax. And that climax looks like a resolution and an answer to many 'higher' problems." It is all the more significant that Herzog here is talking to himself, not to his analyst. Psychoanalysis has become part of personal style. In some of these "sessions," Herzog invokes the master, as when he records his guilt about being an apparition to Marco: "This particular sensitivity about meeting and parting had to be tamed. Such trembling sorrow—he tried to think what term Freud had for it: partial return of repressed traumatic material ultimately traceable to the death instinct?—should not be imparted to children, not that tremulous lifelong swoon of death. This same emotion, as Herzog the student was aware, was held to be the womb of cities, heavenly as well as earthly, mankind being unable to part with its beloved or its dead in this world or the next." But to Herzog, holding his daughter, the emotion is "tyranny." The first half of this idea comes largely from Freud's "Mourning and Melancholia," which is actually mentioned later in the novel when Herzog thinks that "the metabolic wastes of fatigue (he was fond of these physiological explanations; this one came from Freud's essay Mourning and Melancholia) made him temporarily light-hearted, even gay."

Though mentioned only in passing in *Herzog*, "Mourning and Melancholia" is more prominent in the manuscripts, elaborately pondered in a few versions. *"Dear Dr. Freud,"* the depressive Herzog writes in a letter, *"I have recently* in a dark hour *studied your essay on Mourning and Melancholia, as well as the papers of your colleague Dr. Abraham. . . .* As you might imagine I did not *read your essay by accident. Man prays in our religion (or former religion) for a 'new heart.' Radical determinism like yours offers no place for new hearts. But why else would anyone pray or seek light?"* To seeking light through prayer Freud would hardly be responsive, so Herzog pursues the therapeutic line: *"The depressive character is narcissistic. It fears the disappearance of the beloved. Above all terrors it places the terror of abandonment and naked solitude. So with secret hate it cuts off the deserters. Who then reappears within—introjected as you say in your jargon. Then the voice of the love slain speaks continually within, and the depressive abuses and criticizes himself. You say then that the depressive is often able to state the truth about himself quite reliably and accurately, though he often overstates the case, and you add—it must have been irresistable—that it is odd to think that insights should be the result of disease. Or, truthfulness is a consequence of disease. But* my dear man, I am really very fond of that tart old man, *let us go back a bit. Is it possible that some people are born with a greater metaphysical terror than others, with less sheath or with [less] power to apprehend the inhuman and the void? William James makes room in his system for such types, whom he calls 'tender-minded.' . . . However I am grateful to you for certain information, such as that the melancholic is abnormal in stripping his libido so rapidly from the deserting lover. Suffering from love yet intolerably cruel. . . . Have however some singular power that prevents me from laying my head docilely under your sober shade. One of these Moseses of whom you wrote—called meek."* The prime clinical point is made briefly by Edvig in the novel; in manuscript we see Herzog virtually savoring the Freudian wisdom. But with reservations, for Herzog rejects a priori Freud's "radical determinism" as he resists the illusion of total explanation in the diagnosis. He sees just how his reaction to his recent marital disaster has to do with "abandonment" (associated with fear of abandonment by the mother in the earlier versions, as in Freud). He concurs that sickness can be the blow that brings truth, but he attributes part of his depression to metaphysical causes, causes in the nature of things, preferring to include James's tender-mindedness as a necessary element in the explanation, thereby converting sickness into a form of ordinary consciousness. Freud's tartness needs sweetening; even when Bellow is accepting him, it is only a partial acceptance. But if *Herzog* shows how seriously Bellow can take Freud, *The Last Analysis,* written at about the same time, shows that farcical reduction of the claims of psychoanalysis was not far away. Herzog's "singular power," his non-analyzable soul, will never let him rest comfortably with Freud. As if to underscore his tenderminded perception, one more amenable to humanistic comprehension, Herzog signs off, somewhat obscurely, as a meek Moses. The reference is to Freud's *Moses and Monotheism,* which posits two Moses figures who are made to become one: first, the masterful, violent Egyptian who worshipped Aton, and, second, the patient, "meek" Midianite who worshipped Jahve. Freud's book is fascinating but atypical in the sense that, as Rieff puts it, "Freud acknowledges that civilization can be moved by spiritual as well as instinctual discontents." The book is indeed ingenious but eccentric, for against virtually all canons of evidence, it imposes the Oedipal pattern as clearly as in *Totem and Taboo.* Our contemporary Moses does not make much of it.

Though Herzog tells Dr. Freud that he is *"immersed in your Collected Papers,"* though snatches of Freudian language appear in many places in Bellow, usually seriously (sometimes comically, e.g., Hoberly's unrequited love is now called "hysterical dependency" though Bellow recognizes the reality of *an* unconscious, of repression, of the psychological importance of childhood, of filial ambivalence, of behaviour conceived as conflict, nevertheless he can accept Freudianism as at best a partial explanation. Yet he too wants man to be the masculine achiever, and he sees sensuality as a temptation along the way; he too defines woman too quickly in terms of sensuality, and he fears too readily that he will be weakened by her. He too is puzzled by what "they want," though he has a much more contemporary sense of how the intellectual and sensual actually do mix in women. And Bellow is taken by that most Freudian of fables, the ant and the grasshopper. "The ant was once the hero, but now the grasshopper is the whole show," laments Govinda Lal (*Mr. Sammler's Planet*). Few people, it seems to Bellow, are willing to undergo the necessary renunciation which civilization demands. Immediate gratification has submerged higher purpose. For this perversion of his instinctual system, Freud is not responsible. Charlie Citrine is described by the post-Freudian analyst Ellenbogen as "an ant longing to be a grasshopper" (*HG*). Not so, as a Freudian would understand. Perhaps the most enduring instance of Freud's influence on Bellow is the novelist's contempt for grasshopper culture. But, for Bellow, the Freudian instinctual system does not offer a strong enough moral counter to the demands of this culture. There is a lack of autonomy. Bellow sees that Freud wished to preserve human nature from cultural determinism, but he does not want to substitute for it a biological determinism. In a wise rabbinic commentary, it is suggested that God did not say "And it was good" after creating man because man's nature was not determined. The poets of *Genesis* knew what Freud did not, the pull of moral indeterminancy. Bellow possesses this knowledge.

Women in Saul Bellow's Novels

Ada Aharoni

Some critics have asserted that Saul Bellow, throughout his novels, has
failed to describe convincing women. One of these is Leslie Fiedler, who
observes: "Indeed, the whole of Bellow's work is singularly lacking a real
or vivid female character; where women are introduced, they appear as
nympholeptic fantasies, peculiarly unconvincing" (*Love and Death in the
American Novel*). And John Clayton remarks in relation to *Herzog,* "The
women are creations of Herzog's masochistic imagination, not 'real' at
all." It is true that Bellow's artistic technique imposes some limitations on
his portrayal of women characters, as we mainly perceive them through
the minds of his male protagonists who often overshadow them; and because the narrators are men generally going through various existential crises, the female characters in comparison, often do not have the same depth
of emotional, moral, and intellectual complexity as the heroes or anti-he-
roes. Furthermore, we sometimes get the impression that Bellow is more
interested to illuminate certain societal attitudes towards women rather
than to fully delineate their characters.

However, having said that, the fact remains that Bellow through his
thirty-eight years of writing, from *Dangling Man* (1944) to *The Dean's December* (1982), has given us a vast and rich gallery of convincing and vivid
women of all kinds. His female characters are active, alive, creative and
outspoken. They are shown for the most part, as forging meaningful lives
for themselves, struggling, working, searching, growing and achieving.

From *Studies in American Jewish Literature,* no. 3, edited by Daniel Walden. © 1983
by *Studies in American Jewish Literature.*

There are modern "new" women and traditional old-world women, brilliant women and shallow materialistic ones, aging women who are trying to remain "girls" and young women who try to appear older, sensitive and unsensitive women, kind and cruel ones—in one phrase—a whole world peopled by not only men but also by women. Some are two-dimensional and some are three-dimensional, but they're for the most part convincing characters vibrating with life. As it would take much more scope than this paper to describe fully the major types of women throughout Bellow's fiction, I have chosen to limit my analysis to a few of the central female characters appearing at different periods of his writing, and will especially dwell on Madeleine Herzog, who through her character and behaviour exemplifies Bellow's masterful treatment of the characterization of women. This will also enable the tracing of the particular growth and development in the depiction of the female situation appearing throughout Bellow's works.

Dangling Man, Bellow's first novel, is written in the diary form, and we see the central female character, the way her husband, Joseph, sees her and experiences her. Iva, therefore, remains two-dimensional, as we never hear her speak in her own voice, but we learn enough about her to give us a clear idea of her type of personality and her situation as a woman. Iva is young and energetic, and she dearly cherishes her independence. She works as a librarian, and is supportive of Joseph when he is unemployed and waiting for his call-up in the army. She suggests that instead of searching for a new employment, Joseph should use the time to complete writing his book on Diderot, and that in the meantime they could live on her salary. Joseph is enthusiastic about this, and grateful to Iva, but that is when their troubles begin.

Living on his wife's salary constantly gives Joseph the disagreeable feeling that he is "kept" by her. The sensation is further rubbed in by confrontations with her family who seem to accuse him of living at their daughter's expense. He is also confronted with embarrassing situations, as with the bank manager who suspiciously refuses to let him cash Iva's paycheck. Here we feel Bellow is investigating what happens when the woman in the family becomes the breadwinner, and he is critically weighing the repercussions. This new situation adds to the tensions accumulated between Iva and Joseph in the past, and their relationship becomes endangered. One of the major sources of their misunderstanding was that Joseph had looked down on Iva's "superficial" interests such as: "clothes, appearances, furniture, light entertainment, mystery stories, the attraction of fashion magazines." He desperately tries to change her, and the more he tries, the more she resents it and rebels. We feel that Iva, after her long hours amid books and periodicals at the library, needs to relax at home with some lighter kind of reading and entertainment. But Joseph does not understand this. He reasons with himself that if he has not succeeded in changing Iva's tastes it is because women "were not equipped by training to resist such things . . . you might teach them to admire *Walden* but never convert them to wearing old clothes." According to Joseph, women behave the "superfluous" way they do, simply because they have not been taught better. At this point, there is no attempt on his part as yet to understand Iva in terms of individual taste and in terms of a woman's own inner life. What is wrong in liking furniture, clothes, appearances and even mystery stories? Why should Iva be built on the model of the intellectual he would like her to be? However, before the end of the book, Bellow will make his protagonist's view of women evolve during the seven months' span of his diary writing.

In her resentment of his attitude, Iva had gradually become estranged from him, and Joseph turns to another woman, Kitty Daumler, who becomes his mistress. However, in the course of his introspective exploration, when he is revising the whole meaning of the concept of "freedom," it becomes clear to Joseph that "A compact with one woman puts beyond reach what others might give us to enjoy." Through this new insight, Joseph gains in knowledge not only of himself but also of Iva. According to Martin Buber, whom Bellow admires, "in order to be able to go out to the other you must have the starting place, you must have been, you must be, with yourself." It is only when Joseph, through his introspective search, has been "with himself" that he can understand Iva, the other, better. The "other" or the "thou" in Buber is different than in Simone de Beauvoir, who sees in the term "other" something derogatory—not only separate, but subsidiary and alien.

At that point, it penetrates Joseph's consciousness fully that Iva might not want to be changed, that her freedom is as dear to her as his is to himself, and he comes to the crucial realization that the ultimate quest for freedom, being common to all people, is a unifying element in human relationships. "The quest," Joseph writes in his diary, "is one and the same," and his conclusion is that because "the desire for pure freedom" is the same, "the differences in our personal histories, which hitherto meant so much to us . . . become of minor importance." He admits that in trying to reform Iva's taste, he had "dominated her for years."

Thus, having gained a new insight into the essence of the concept of freedom, Joseph has more understanding and respect for Iva. He comments in his diary: "It was not evident that Iva did not want to be towed. Those dreams inspired by Burckhardt's great ladies of the Renaissance and the no less profound Augustan women were in my head, not hers. Eventually I learned that Iva could not live in my infatuations." Joseph now understands that his aspirations for Iva, were a response to masculine-centered values. Bellow brings his protagonist to a full realization that Iva is not only his wife, but a person in her own right, with tastes of her own and a personality of her own, and that he has to accept her the way she is. Thus at the outset of his brilliant literary career, Bellow already clearly shows his concern with relationships between men and women, and with the depiction of the female situation in modern life.

Ten years later, in *Herzog* (1964), which is considered by most critics to be Bellow's masterpiece, we have a fascinating psychological study in Madeleine Herzog. Unlike Iva, Madeleine is three-dimensional, though she too is mainly described through the male protagonist's perception. We get an accurate and vivid description of how Herzog experiences her, but we also clearly see what she is like, for as Opdahl comments: "Although Bellow gives us only Herzog's view of Madeleine . . . the thoroughness of his portrayal of Herzog is itself a check on Herzog's view." In his frantic attempt to be fair to her and to view her in an objective way, Herzog gives us a full, convincing and vivid portrayal of Madeleine. Through his perception, we can not only clearly visualize Madeleine, but even see her side of the story too. Since it is Herzog, the hurt ex-husband who tells the story of his painful divorce with Madeleine, whom he still loves, his word carries a good deal of weight, and yet, underneath the male's point of view we can also discern that of the female.

Madeleine, who is one of the most interesting of Bellow's woman characters, is portrayed as brilliant, beautiful, ambitious, restless, aggressive and outspoken. And throughout the novel, Herzog who is painfully struggling to get rid of his passion for her, is in a constant conflict between his striving to be an objective observer, and the subjective view of the hurt ex-husband who has been abandoned for another man. Trying hard to be fair to her, he admits that she has "great charm, and beauty of person also, and a brilliant mind," but he often cannot help slipping back to his subjective view. He starts: "Quite objectively, however, she was a beauty . . . the bangs concealed a forehead of a considerable intellectual power," then he subjectively continues: "the will of a demon, or else outright mental disorder." He admires not only her intelligence, her beauty, and her will-power, but also "the perfection of her self-control. She never hesitated . . . it gave him a headache merely to look at her."

In addition to the protagonist's view, Madeleine is also characterized through her relations with the various characters in the novel, and what they say about her. It is significant that most of the women in the novel admire Madeleine. Geraldine Portnoy says of her: "She is so vivacious, intelligent, and such a charmer. . . . It is extremely exciting to talk with her, she gives a sense of a significant encounter—with life—a beautiful, brilliant person with a fate of her own." Joanna Russ comments that in general, "a woman who competes with men, finally becomes—have we seen this figure before?—a bitch. Again." And indeed, Madeleine is called a bitch by several men, who at the same time all admire her for her strength of character. For instance, the lawyer Sandor Himmelstein tells Herzog that she is "a strong-minded bitch, terrifically attractive. Loves to make up her mind. Once decided, decided forever. What a will power. It's a type," and he argues with Herzog: "she's less of a whore than most. We're all whores in this world, and don't you forget it." As a child, Madeleine had been sexually abused, which partly explains her sexual frigidity towards Herzog; but Herzog prefers to consider it "bitchiness" on her part. "She's built a wall of Russian books around herself . . . in my bed," he complains, and resentfully feels that her studies have invaded their most intimate privacy—their very conjugal bed. At that point Herzog had not yet realized the full impact Madeleine's "books" would have on their lives.

There is a basic antagonism between their marriage and Madeleine's studies. As many modern intellectual women (we are told that she was a brilliant Radcliffe graduate), Madeleine finds that her family life does not give her sufficient scope, challenge or satisfaction, and she feels the deep need for further growth and for pursuing a career. Through Herzog's narration we can see that Madeleine too is going through a crisis and "rethinking everything." In her, we can perceive a woman in conflict who is having a hard time living with a husband she does not love, and whom she tries to avoid. At the beginning of her marriage, she probably had hopes that Herzog would make some room for her career beside his own. But Herzog wants her to forego her own intellectual pursuits, to help him with his book on the Romantics. He feels hurt, thwarted, cheated and frustrated when she shows no inclination to do so, and goes on pursuing her own studies on Russian philosophy. Madeleine, at that point, has ceased to view herself as a function of the needs of a man who fails to satisfy her own deepest need.

This should have been a red light for Herzog to realize that something was wrong in their relationship, but he continues to show no interest in her studies, and to regard them as if she were studying against him. When his friend Shapiro asks him what the title of her doctoral thesis is, he admits that he doesn't know what her research is about, but only vaguely knows that it has something to do with "Slavonic languages," or Russian religious history (I guess)." Yet he expects her to know everything concerning the new book he is writing on the Romantics, and wants her to actively participate in it, under his own name of course. We know from him that he not only regards Madeleine a "brilliant mind," but that he has great faith in her probing and intelligent professional judgment. In several instances his male-chauvinism is blatant. In one of these, he admits that he had condescendingly "endured" her lectures on her research subject "many times, and far into the night. He didn't dare say he was sleepy" because, he continues, "he had to discuss knotty points of Rousseau and Hegel with her," as he "relied completely on her intellectual judgments." He fools her into thinking that he is really listening to her plea for a second opinion about her research—when his mind is far away from anything she has to say—only because he needs to discuss his own ideas and intellectual interests with her! We never hear about what Madeleine is talking to him "far into the night," but we have the precise details of what he needed to discuss with her. And then Herzog is surprised and deeply hurt when Madeleine leaves him for Valentine Gersbach who shows much more interest in her as a person and an individual.

Shapiro's visit to the Herzogs should also have been a warning sign of how lacking and unfair Herzog's attitude is to his wife's studies. It is only through Herzog's remembrance of Madeleine's conversation with Shapiro that we hear about her intellectual interests, and are surprised to hear how well-read she is and what vast knowledge she has, ranging over: the Russian Church, Tikhom Zadonsky, Dostoevsky, Herzen, the Revolution of 1848, Bakunin, Kropotkin, Comfort, Poggioli, Rozanov, Soloviev and Joseph de Maistre. Shapiro who is himself a learned scholar, is very impressed by Madeleine's expertise in her field, her vast knowledge and quick mind. Herzog relates that Shapiro was delighted with Madeleine and thought her intelligent and learned, and he sadly admits to himself: "well, she is." She and Shapiro conversed excitedly, and laughed gaily during their exchange of ideas, which made Herzog jealous, resenting the fact that she never laughed in this carefree way with him, and that they "found each other exceedingly stimulating."

In his flashback of the visit, Herzog admits that Madeleine, "stuck away in the woods," was avid for scholarly conversation, and that she would naturally find some interest in Shapiro who was well-read in her field, and yet "he watched his wife, on whom he doted (with a troubled, angry heart), as she revealed the wealth of her mind to Shapiro." He bitterly describes this revealing of her mind, almost as if it were an indecent act or a bodily striptease. In his jealousy, he considers everything pertaining to his wife, including her mind, as his exclusive possession, which should be revealed only to him, and not to any Shapiro. Reflecting on this, Herzog later admits to himself, that he had never been as interested in Madeleine's subject of research as Shapiro was. He relates that Madeleine, when she had "enough confidence in Shapiro to speak freely knowing it would be appreciated, genuinely"—which implied a contrast with his own attitude—seemed "bursting with ideas and feelings."

Madeleine, watching the sullen Herzog, was hurt that he did not join in the lively conversation, and only sat there "like a clunk, bored, resentful," as if he wanted to prove that "he didn't respect her intelligence." Her offended look passed over her husband, as if complaining that he disdained her work and never really listened to her, "he wanted to shine all the time," and resented the fact that it was her turn to shine. When Shapiro complimented her on her knowledge, "she was flattered, happy," and hoped her husband would change his attitude towards her studies when he felt that other people deeply appreciated her knowledge. But here again we witness a conflict between Herzog's objectivity and subjectivity. Even in retrospect he still tends to regard Shapiro and Mady's intellectual exchanges as mere "learned badinage," or small talk. In his jealousy, he is convinced that Shapiro is more interested in Madeleine's physical beauty than by her mind, and hints that it is mainly her beautiful "behind" that he is really involved in.

When Shapiro suggests that they move to Chicago for Madeleine's studies, Herzog is infuriated, "Fill your big mouth with herring, Shapiro! . . . and mind your own fucking business." He cannot envisage the possibility of moving to satisfy his wife's ambition for a career. His contemptuous attitude towards her studies drives Madeleine to pursue them still more intently, to prove that she can succeed. Herzog keenly resents that and describes it as a cruel and exaggerated competition between them:

> I understood that Madeleine's ambition was to take my place in the learned world. To overcome me. She was reaching her final elevation, as queen of the intellectuals, the castiron bluestocking. And your friend Herzog writhing under this sharp elegant heel. . . . Madeleine, by the way, lured me out of the learned world, got in herself, slammed the door, and is still in there, gossiping about me.

As if there were only one place in the academic world, and that she has to throw him out, before she can usurp that place! Her knowledge is so threatening to him, that he would much have preferred to keep her unlearned. From his point of view, if she has a thirst for knowledge he is ready to introduce her into his own intellectual pursuits (and exploit her intelligence for his own professional interests), and does not understand why she does not accept his benevolent offer, and does not discard her career in favour of his.

Some critics have found Madeleine unsympathetic, cold, unstable and neurotic. Leslie Fiedler, in *Love and Death in the American Novel,* says that Madeleine "seems a nightmare projection bred by baffled malice, rather than a realized woman; and Herzog's passionate involvement with her remains, therefore, unconvincing." But Herzog's passion for Madeleine is the psycho-center of the novel, and if it were unconvincing, *Herzog* would not have been the masterpiece it has been acclaimed to be; neither would have Bellow received the Nobel Prize for literature, when his main opus is deemed to be "unconvincing." It is, on the contrary, only because Madeleine is such a lifelike character that Herzog's passionate involvement with her is convincing. As to her seeming "cold" and "unstable"—these are certainly the symptoms of the unfulfilled and unsatisfied woman, who feels she is not given the opportunity to "grow," and much of her frustrations stem from the fact that Herzog thwarts her intellectual drives and goals. Furthermore, certain critics, such as John Clayton, seem to overlook the fact that in stressing only the negative aspects of her character, they have probably been influenced by the hurt ex-husband view.

Eventually, Herzog comes to realize that Madeleine must have suffered from his antagonistic attitude towards her studies and intellectual goals. The fear that her need for intellectual fulfilment was a compensation and a substitute for her lack of emotional fulfilment with him, had probably unconsciously caused him to be so contemptuous and antagonistic towards her studies and aspirations for a career. When he comes to see Edvig, and the psychiatrist asks him why he supposed her crisis happened, Herzog recognizes that it might have been caused by his contempt of her intellectual pursuits, which had given her the feeling that he was "disrespectful of her rights as a person."

Yet, he persists in describing Madeleine as a domineering and cruel woman; but here again, his depiction is so extensive, that underlying his version, we also get hers. He recalls that she describes him as a tyrant, and we see that to her he must have appeared just as cruel. Jack Ludwig rightly notes that Bellow must certainly be aware that Herzog is not much more moral than his Mady and Gersbach. Mady writes to Herzog complaining that when she was in a room with him, he "seemed to swallow and gulp up all the air and left nothing for her to breathe." She also resented the fact that he had adventures with other women, and as we learn from Herzog's conversation with Aunt Zelda, her accusations were well based.

In his confrontation with Mady, Herzog seems to have wanted a wife, who, like his mother, was a Yiddishe mama who would have lived only for him and the children. But he had one of those in his first wife, Daisy, and he had left her precisely because of this: "I gave up the shelter of an orderly, purposeful, lawful existence because it bored me." In a way, he is getting the same treatment from Mady as he himself has given to Daisy; but it hurts much more when you are the one who is abandoned, than when you abandon. He also regrets his past attitude towards Sono, his Japanese mistress. He had been responsible for having kept her from returning to Japan, and made her disobey her father. Yet, when she had a severe attack of pneumonia for a whole month, he had not even gone to see her once. Thus Herzog comes to realize that he is not the only victim who has been caused to suffer rejection at the hand of a partner, but that he too had inflicted suffering of the same kind on various women.

Madeleine held a different conception of a woman's life than either Daisy, Sono or Herzog—yet he did not grasp that, and was pained and bewildered by her attitude. Feeling that he had given her all that she could want, he considered himself "Madeleine's particular benefactor. He had done everything for her—everything!" Mady keenly resents his patronising attitude, and during one of their quarrels in the Berkshires, she cries out desperately:

> So now we're going to hear how you SAVED me. Let's hear it again. What a frightened puppy I was. How I wasn't strong enough to face life. But you gave me LOVE, from your big heart, and rescued me from the priests. Yes, cured me of menstrual cramps by servicing me so good. You SAVED me. You SACRIFICED your freedom. I took you away from Daisy and your son, and your Japanese screw. Your important time and money and attention.

From her indignant outburst, we gather that Herzog had been cramming down her throat that she should be thankful to him as her generous benefactor, a long time before the disruption takes place; until Mady could no longer take it. Another interesting point to notice here, is the development in the characterization. Unlike Iva, we often hear Mady talking in her own voice. Her sharp repartee and her witty dialogues and arguments add an in-depth dimension to her characterization.

Why did Madeleine who is in her early twenties, want to marry Herzog, her forty-four year-old professor? She probably saw in him a father-figure who would replace her own father whom she had lost to the theater. She also may have converted to Catholicism for the same reason, seeing in the Monsignor a father-figure with whom she could freely talk and confess herself—a close relationship she had never had with any of her parents. But we saw how Herzog responded to her need of talking—by tricking her into thinking that he was listening to her, so that she would accept to help him with his research.

Whereas Herzog disregarded Mady's intellectual aspirations, he complained to her that she neglected her household duties in Ludeyville. Mady retorts that she could not cope with the vast housework in the large derelict mansion, "it needs four servants and you want me to do all the work." He resented the fact that she did not accept the subservient position he wanted to allocate her, and felt that he was "a broken down monarch of some kind." This is reminiscent of Henderson's attitude towards his wife, Lily: "I didn't like to see her behave and carry on like the lady of the house; because I, the sole heir of the famous name and estate, am a bum, and she is not a lady—but merely my wife—merely my wife." Thus we see that domineering men, and the attitude to women as second class citizens abound among Bellow's protagonists. There is also a kind of bafflement before the essence and definition of woman. Herzog, for instance, regards them as lurid kinds of vampires: "will never understand what women want. What do they want? They eat green salad and drink human blood." In much the same vein, Tommy Wilhelm, the protagonist of *Seize the Day,* exclaims that he will never understand "women or money"—the implication being that money and women are on the same level: inanimate, material matter and mere commodities.

After two years of marriage, Madeleine cannot cope anymore with Herzog's domineering and patronizing. It is interesting to compare Madeleine's attitude to the divorce with that of Herzog—whereas she states in relief that the divorce was "the first time in her life she knew clearly what she was doing. Until now it was all confusion"—Herzog went to pieces. The climax of his struggle to overcome his passion occurs when he goes to shoot Madeleine and her lover in Chicago. However, when he watches through the window he sees a peaceful domestic scene: Mady washing dishes and cleaning the kitchen, and Valentine tenderly bathing Junie. This peaceful harmony brings a change in his attitude; he is confronted with an actual situation, two people in love living peaceably together, and not the monsters he had expected to find. He concludes: "Let the child find life," and as to the lovers, "if, even in that embrace of lust and treason, they had life and nature on their side, he would step quietly aside." He has arrived at the full realization that Madeleine did not love him, "Madeleine refused to be married to him, and people's wishes have to be respected. Slavery is dead."

After he has succeeded in uprooting Madeleine from his system, Phoebe asks him if he wants Madeleine back, and he answers frankly: "I wish her a busy, useful, pleasant, dramatic life. Including *love*. The best people fall in love, and she's one of the best." Herzog has finally succeeded in freeing himself of his obsession for Madeleine, and in so doing, he has given us one of the best feminine portraits in Bellow's works. Madeleine emerges as a "new woman" who makes her own choices, and who ultimately takes her destiny into her own hands rather than being defeated by a patriarchal society. She embodies in her character and her actions the "free" woman who struggles to achieve her chance of growth and her goal of an independent career, as well as her goal of finding real love. Her true-to-life portrayal, her authenticity and her vividness, make her one of the best feminine portraits of her kind in modern American literature.

Ramona, the woman Herzog becomes involved with, after Madeleine has left him, is quite a different character. She combines the characteristics of the conventional Jewish wife: warm, gentle, loving, an excellent cook, and has genuine family feelings—with those of the modern woman: she is independent, hard-working, intellectual and sexual. Herzog considers her a "sexual masterpiece," and he compares her to the Egyptian goddess of fecundity, calling her a "priestess of Isis." He also greatly admires her independent spirit: "She struggled, she fought. In this world, to be a woman who took matters into her own hands!" Ramona has already arrived at the goal of full personhood that Mady was aspiring to. She has already structured her life according to her own vision of authenticity, and Herzog admires her for it—when it is not at *his* expense that she has to achieve it! He also admires her wisdom, and in one of his mental letters, recognizing that she has done a great deal for him in striving to give him self-confidence again, he writes: "Dear Ramona—Very dear Ramona. I like you very much—dear to me, a true friend . . . you have the complete wisdom."

Ramona owns a flower shop which she runs herself, and has in her very personality a "fragrant" quality. Thinking of her, Herzog praises her, "you're lovely, fragrant, sexual, good to touch—everything." Nonetheless, there is a mock-heroic note in his description of the elaborate way Ramona dresses up for their sexual encounters, with her black laced underclothes and her alluring postures which make him think of a Spanish dancer or "devodorada," "she entered a room provocatively, swaggering slightly, one hand touching her thigh, as though she carried a knife in her garter belt." The mention of the knife shows that his traumatic experience with Madeleine makes him regard women—even warm, gentle and affectionate Ramona—as castrators. Typically, he is also suspicious of her ideology. She preached *"mens sana in corpore sano,"*—a healthy soul is in a healthy body—and had deeply absorbed the teachings of Marcuse, N. O. Brown and the neo-Freudians who believed the body is the instrument of the soul. She tells Herzog that the art of love is one of the most sublime achievements of the soul, and tries to teach him how to renew the spirit through the flesh—"the true and only temple of the spirit." On the whole, however, Ramona delights Herzog, and he cries in admiration: "Bless the girl! What pleasure she gave him. All her ways satisfied him—her French—Russian—Argentine—Jewish ways." At the end of the novel, we find Herzog preparing a meal for Ramona and picking flowers for her, things he had never done before for any of the other women.

It is interesting to note that whereas Madeleine complains that she cannot cope with the household chores in Ludeyville, when Herzog watches her through the window in Chicago with Valentine, she is washing the dishes. In Ramona's apartment, Herzog himself wants to wash the dishes after dinner, for, he explains, "there is something about washing dishes that calms me." And at the end of the novel, when the reformed, and out-of-crisis Herzog invites Ramona to dinner in his own house where he has cooked a good meal for her—he thinks: "She would help him with the dishes." The point that Bellow is obviously making is, that when the relationship between the couple is harmonious, the household chores do not represent a problem. Ultimately, in comparing the two women, and their situation in the novel—whereas Madeleine, in Evelyn Torton Beck's terms, refuses to inhabit the "background" of her husband's "foreground" anymore—Ramona does not have to enter Herzog's background, as she has attained her own foreground. Bellow demonstrates that beautifully ("The Many Faces of Eve: Women, Yiddish, and I. B. Singer," *Studies in American Jewish Literature,* edited by Daniel Walden).

In *Humboldt's Gift,* we have a description of two main kinds of women, those, like Ramona, who are "the ultimate source of nourishment and comfort for men;" and those as Herzog would like us to think Madeleine was—women who are, in Sanford Radnor's terms, "deceitful depleters" ("The Woman Savior in *Humboldt's Gift,*" Saul Bellow Journal 1 [1981]). But the most independent woman character we have had in any of Bellow's novels until now, in my opinion, is Minna Corde, in his last

novel, *The Dean's December*. In Minna, who is a world-famous astrono-
mer, Bellow gives us a lifelike model and a convincing illustration of what
a struggling, working, creating, "new" woman is. But Minna is such a
fascinating character, that she deserves a whole study to herself. Let me
just make a last observation: from Iva to Minna, Bellow has come a long
way in his depiction of women characters, and I for one would not be surprised if his next protagonist would be a woman.

Herzog: A Reading from the Dark Side

Jonathan Wilson

Herzog is a novel about a man freeing himself from a paralyzing obsession with his ex-wife. Almost all of the action takes place inside Moses Herzog's head as he spends a week and a half in feverish thought going over the breakup of his marriage and all its contingent elements: betrayals, lies, child-custody problems, alimony, untrustworthy shrinks, bad friends, deceitful lawyers, conspiring relatives. Painful stuff all of it—or is it?

The opening line of _Herzog_ gives us an indication that things may, in fact, be changing for Bellow's burdened and struggling heroes. "If I am out of my mind it's all right with me," thinks Moses Herzog, which seems to be good news as it certainly has not been all right for the five heroes who have preceded him in Bellow's canon. From Joseph through Henderson, a craziness induced by crisis (and vice versa) rends Bellow's heroes to quite devastating effect, but although Moses Herzog suffers in much the same way as his forebears (almost everyone he knows cheats and betrays him), he seems to be enjoying himself. As he himself puts it, "Moses, suffering, suffered in style."

It is hard to know what precipitated this slight but important shift in Bellow's realization of his hero's consciousness and in its relation to the matter of his life—perhaps Bellow simply grew tired of all that endless striving—but its effect is to remove a great weight from Bellow's later fiction. "Was he a clever man or an idiot?" is Herzog's opening question to himself, a familiar one for a Bellow hero to ask, but the answer Herzog

From _On Bellow's Planet: Readings from the Dark Side._ © 1985 by Associated University Presses, Inc. Fairleigh Dickinson University Press, 1985.

provides in the novel is less common. What a shock it is to hear Herzog describe himself as a "child-man," "an eager, hasty, self-intense and comical person," "a frail, hopeful lunatic" suffering from "monstrous egotism," and to see him ironically present himself as a "pure heart in the burlap of innocence" with whom "everyone must be indulgent."

Before the critic has sharpened his pencil, Herzog is bringing himself "to consider his character. What sort of character was it? Well, in the modern vocabulary, it was narcissistic; it was masochistic; it was anachronistic." [Elsewhere], I somberly deduced these characteristics in Bellow's other heroes and suggested that they contributed to the bleak atmosphere of Bellow's novels. But here is Herzog, evincing a detached gaiety, hanging his personality on the line, "knowing" everything about himself, and, apparently, not giving a damn.

Periodically in the novel, Herzog enacts a session of self-analysis that seems to parody a real analysis. Lying supine on a couch in his Manhattan apartment, Herzog apparently instructs his mind to roll free. But, unlike, say, the analysis in that other great self-consumptive novel of the 1960s, *Portnoy's Complaint,* Herzog's presentation of self is altogether protective.

> Resuming his self-examination, he admitted that he had been a bad husband—twice. Daisy, his first wife, he had treated miserably. Madeleine, his second, had tried to do *him* in. To his son and his daughter he was a loving but bad father. To his own parents he had been an ungrateful child. To his country, an indifferent citizen. To his brothers and sister, affectionate but remote. With his friends an egotist. With love, lazy. With brightness, dull. With power, passive. With his own soul, evasive.

All this sounds reasonable enough when set in the measured tones of Bellow's ingenuous protagonist (as opposed to the hysterical ones of Roth's Alexander Portnoy). Moreover, although we learn that Herzog is "[s]atisfied with his own severity [and] positively enjoying the hardness and factual rigor of his judgment," we never feel like pillorying Herzog either for his familial irresponsibility or his self-satisfied posing. Herzog soon emerges as "our hero," a beleaguered, sympathetic, attractive personality. Bellow carefully manipulates our response to Herzog's self-criticism and we tend to feel—well, let's just wait and see what these brothers, sisters, friends, and ex-wives are *really* like before we decide who treated whom miserably.

Herzog's emotional problems seem to engage him on some upper level of his mind where they no longer hurt. But it is the way in which he has got them up there that proves to be central to our understanding of the novel. Herzog's marital crisis has somehow "heightened his perceptions," and it has also stimulated him in other ways.

> What I seem to do, thought Herzog, is to inflame myself with my own drama, with ridicule, failure, denunciation, distortion, to inflame myself voluptuously, aesthetically, until I reach a sexual climax. And that climax looks like a resolution and an answer to many higher problems.

Conceiving of himself as an "industry that manufacture[s] personal history," Herzog is an essentially autonomous institution imaginatively geared up by his personal crises and sustained by the wildly complex intellectual figurations that his sexual sublimations throw up. He is, in fact, Bellow's most sophisticated alchemist of crisis: his narrative turns the dross of a tawdry and troubled personal life into a platform for the discussion of everything from German existentialism to Russian mysticism, Calvinism, and Black Muslims, and everyone from Montaigne and Pascal to Kant, Fichte, Nietzsche, Spengler, Heidegger, Eisenhower, Adlai Stevenson, and Martin Luther King, Jr.

In a lengthy series of highly charged mental letters, Herzog writes to "the newspapers, to people in public life, to friends and relatives . . . to the dead, his own obscure dead, and finally the famous dead." His performance is quite dazzling; thoughts, associations, grand and petty ideas run, leap, pound, and tingle through his brain with astonishing rapidity. It is all wonderful stuff for the reader—but are we supposed to take Herzog's ideas seriously, or more seriously than his emotional troubles?

If one idea is uppermost in Herzog's mind, it seems to be that people who live by ideas need debunking. Herzog's own ideas, as he acknowledges, are the flotsam and jetsam of a troubled mind—superfluities, distractions. The intellectual motions that he goes through are graceful, humorous, to the point—*"Dear Doktor Professor Heidegger, I should like to know what you mean by the expression 'the fall into the quotidian.' When did this fall occur? Where were we standing when it happened?"*—but they are a sideshow.

Herzog's ultimate goal is a kind of transcendental peace, an inner and outer quietness: he yearns to still the babble of tongues inside him, to rid his mind of clutter and to exorcise the ghosts of his disastrous marriage. If doing so takes him by way of nineteenth- and twentieth-century German existential theories that he must ponder and discredit before he can dismiss, then so be it.

In its own way *Herzog* is a *Portnoy's Complaint* for intellectuals. The figures in the nightmare—who also provide the entertainment—are not two lower-middle-class Jewish parents with medieval ideas about propriety and *kashrut,* but a whole set of book-crazy movers and shakers—shrinks, lawyers, and academics who have linked arms in Herzog's head with a band of heavyweight philosophers and theologians. In terms of substance, however, nothing of what these pundits and thinkers have to say is of any deeper relevance to Moses Herzog than Sophie Portnoy's meditations on the uncertain properties of the doughnut are to her wayward son.

If neither Herzog's emotional problems nor his intellectual wrangling solidify into anything more than the shiny, brittle surface of the novel, what is it that gives the book its depth? "My novel," Bellow once wrote, "deals with the humiliating sense that results from the American mixture of private concerns and intellectual interests. . . . To me a significant theme of *Herzog* is the imprisonment of the individual in a shameful and impotent privacy. . . . He comes to realize at last that what he has considered his intellectual privilege has proved to be another form of bondage. Anyone who misses this misses the point of the book." Herzog himself makes the same point another way. "Herzog . . . by accepting the design of a *private life* (approved by those in authority) turned himself into something resembling a concubine." Here, as elsewhere, "private life" and all its attendant sexual wranglings is imaged by Herzog as the outlet for "public" and "political" energies that have been frustrated. In other times a man as smart as Herzog would not have been superfluous.

> What was he hanging around for? To follow this career of *personal relationships* until his strength at last gave out? Only to be a smashing success in the private realm, a king of hearts? Amorous Herzog, seeking love. . . . But this is a female pursuit. This hugging and heartbreak is for women. The occupation of a man is duty, in use, in civility, in politics in the Aristotelian sense.

It is not always an intelligent move to take issue with a living author about the themes of his own book, and indeed *Herzog* does make the point that Bellow claims for it. However, it seems to me that Herzog, cut off as he is from the world of public usefulness, suffers a deeper imprisonment

than that of confinement to the private life. The opposition that Bellow
sets up between private and public worlds—an opposition that he claims
derives from the American refusal to treat intellectual men as responsible
adults who can be trusted with power—actually seems to be a variation of
the more idiosyncratic (and paradoxically more generalized) struggles of
all Bellow's heroes with authority, adulthood, "order," and "civilization."
Herzog, like all his predecessors is doomed by his recalcitrant personality
to forever attack the objects of his own desire. His "intellectual privilege"
may well be a form of bondage but it also proves to be abundant compensation for the terrible paralysis involved in acting out Bellow's version of
the human condition. It is in fact the tension between the familiar "deep
structure" of Bellow's novels and its pyrotechnic surface (the manifestations of Herzog's intellectual privilege) that make *Herzog* at once so frus-
trating and so compelling.

The deep contradictions in Herzog's personality are revealed to us
through his extended ruminations on his personal history. Through them
we learn that, though he is a middle-aged academic who has searched for
order in his life, Herzog has repeatedly acted in such a way as to ensure
that he will find only chaos. Employed in a "perfectly respectable" secure,
tenured, academic position, Herzog has, when we meet him, given up his
job in favor of part-time night-school teaching and daytime intellectual
meandering. Once married to a woman—Daisy—who offered him all the
comforts of an honest bourgeois housewife—"stability, symmetry, order,
containment were Daisy's strengths"—Herzog abandoned her in favor of
the wild and unfaithful Madeleine.

> What actually happened? I gave up the shelter of an orderly,
> purposeful, lawful existence because it bored me, and I felt it
> was simply a slacker's life.

Madeleine, as well as being a Great Bitch, is also the great architect
of chaos in Herzog's life. She bounces checks, refuses to clean up the
house, and betrays Herzog with his best friend, Valentine Gersbach. Irresponsible and extravagant, she is everything that the dull Daisy is not.
Does this make Herzog happy? Not on your life. " 'Jesus Christ,' " he
cries as the checks come back " 'Can't you add! . . . We've got to have a
little order in these surroundings.' " Divorce from Madeleine is as inevitable as was divorce from Daisy. Herzog can no more remain in their company than could Henderson in that of the Arnewi and the Wariri.

Herzog characterizes himself as a softy, a "naive" someone whose
outlook on life is considered by most adults to be excessively childish, and

he partly attributes the breakup of his second marriage to these aspects of his personality. Believing in "truth, friendship, devotion to children," and feeling that he is a man who has "tried to live out marvellous qualities vaguely comprehended," Herzog feels that his "innocent" beliefs and "childish" faith in the ultimate goodness of the world, are under attack from practically all his "adult" and "realistic" friends.

> A *very special sort of lunatic expects to inculcate his principles.*
> Sandor Himmelstein, Valentine Gersbach, Madeleine P. Herzog, Moses himself. *Reality Instructors.* They want to teach you—to punish you with—the lessons of the real.

Oddly, Herzog includes himself in this Augie March-type list of "imposers upon" (*The Adventures of Augie March*), but the novel does not go far in consolidating Herzog's ironies at his own expense. If he is a "Reality Instructor," he is a benign version of the real thing, insisting for the most part that "realism" does not have to be "brutal," that "brotherhood is what makes a man human," and that " 'Man liveth not by Self alone.' "

Herzog's Reality Instructors tend to take the opposite line. They are a hard-nosed lot who believe in "facts." As Sandor Himmelstein, Herzog's lawyer, tells Moses when his client begins to get a little abstract:

> "Don't get highfalutin. I'm talking facts, not shit."
> "And you think a fact is what's nasty."
> "Facts *are* nasty."
> "You think they're true because they're nasty?"
> ". . . Don't give me that hoity-toity. I'm a Kike myself and got my diploma in a stinking night school. Okay? Now let's both knock off this crap dreamy boy."

In the company of the "childish" Herzog, the Reality Instructors in addition to getting angry tend to get paternal and oddly sentimental. Sometimes it seems as if the presence of the "foolish" intellectual alone is enough to bring tears to a Reality Instructor's eyes. Herzog's innocence reminds them of their childhood and this breaks them up, while his "unreality" is so pathetic that it makes a grown man weep.

In one sense the Reality Instructors prove their own case. For, while Herzog goes around reasserting his faith in brotherhood, his "brothers"— Himmelstein; Dr. Edvig, the analyst; Gersbach—are busy giving Herzog some personal instruction in the art of deceit: Himmelstein passes his fees from Herzog on to Madeleine *"to buy clothing"*; Edvig becomes fascinated with Herzog's "in session" descriptions of Madeleine, asks to meet her, and then, captivated, turns against his own patient; while Gersbach's long affair with Madeleine is conducted simultaneously to his holding best-friend status in Herzog's life.

Whose version of reality is the more convincing? The novel as a whole seems to side with the "Reality Instructors"—largely because Herzog's ideas are so forcefully contradicted by his experiences. However, the Reality Instructors are the usual bunch of hypocrites, liars, bitches and know-alls that surround a Bellow hero, and as such they create what we might call a "credibility gap." Moreover, while Herzog tends to categorize them in familiar terms as both "gold" and "shit," there seems, perhaps because a sexual betrayal is involved, to be more than the usual emphasis on the "shit." Madeleine, for example, for all her imperious manner, "masterful conduct," and perfect "Byzantine profile," is, Herzog tells us, "proud but not well-wiped," has a "dirty way" about her, and gives off unpleasant "odors of feminine secretions." Gersbach does not come off much better. He (and who is there to refute Herzog on this?) is a "charlatan, psychopath, with . . . hot phony eyes."

By contrast, Herzog himself comes across as an insightful character—and he is the one with whom we identify and sympathize. Herzog, however, seems alone in his faith in humankind's potential for goodness. Or rather he finds himself in the company of one good man—his friend Lucas Asphalter. Asphalter is the one loyal and trustworthy character in the novel. It is Asphalter who first tells Herzog that he has been betrayed and Asphalter who is always ready to offer Herzog comfort in one form or another—a spare bed, a drink, a sympathetic ear. However, in the manner common to Bellow's characterizations of "good" men, Asphalter is more than passingly odd. A zoologist, Asphalter has become well known in scientific circles for trying to save his favorite monkey Rocco's life by giving him mouth-to-mouth resuscitation. That Rocco was suffering from TB at the time has only added to the "scandal." Thus, on the melioristic side of things, we really have only Herzog to rely on.

Sometimes it seems as if Bellow, the hopeful optimist, through his mouthpiece Herzog, is doing battle with Bellow the novelist and his altogether less-compromising versions of reality. This kind of novelistic friction can produce astonishing results—one might think of Dostoevsky's brilliant argument against his own beliefs in *The Brothers Karamazov*—but in *Herzog* the whole argument as to the true nature of reality (unlike the arguments of "The Grand Inquisitor") seems somehow peripheral to Bellow's larger concerns.

As the novel progresses, it becomes increasingly difficult to take Herzog seriously when he talks about "brotherhood." For he seems to make every effort to live in a self-enclosed world. Herzog's happiest times in the novel come at the end when he is holed up alone in his isolated, rundown country house in the Berkshires. When he scoops up a copy of Rozanov's *Solitaria* (Eugene Henderson's favorite game is solitaire), he seems the happiest man alive. And his happiness is only disturbed when his brother Will arrives and, behaving in a brotherly way, tries to convince Herzog to take a few days convalescence in a hospital (possibly a mental hospital). Herzog is quite happy to be terminally estranged from the world that he inhabits—a fact that calls into question the sincerity of his constant expressions of communal yearning and that undermines the supposedly humanistic vision that critics have discovered in so many Bellow novels.

Herzog's argument with the "Reality Instructors" ultimately comes to seem merely the expression of a much deeper Bellovian conflict: that between what Bellow conceives to be "childish" and "adult," and "feminine" and "male" principles in American society. The reader comes away from *Herzog* with the feeling that Herzog is probably wrong about reality (it is not benign) and therefore correct in his assessments of what most Americans think it takes to be effectual, powerful, and manly in America. That is, the society's values create its own unpleasant reality. Herzog associatively aligns himself with all those whom American "male" realism has excluded from "public" life—most significantly women. However, Herzog is no feminist. He would like women to remain in the "private realm," and he would like men to set him free of it.

In an interview that he gave to *Life* magazine in 1970, Bellow described how writers of his generation

> suffer from the persistent American feeling that the intellectual life is somehow not virile. Artists and Professors like clergymen and librarians, are thought to be female. Our populist tradition requires the artist to represent himself as a man of the people and to conceal his real concern with thought. Maybe that's why we don't have more novels of ideas.

Bellow goes on to suggest that "the powerful hold fiction writers in contempt" because they get no evidence from modern literature that anybody is thinking about significant questions. Seen in this light, *Herzog* seems not so much a defense of supposedly "feminine" and "childish" points of view, but an attempt to appease "the powerful" with big ideas and, paradoxically, to convince them that it is novels of ideas and not novels about fishing and hunting that are truly "manly." Bellow seems to be saying that Herzog and men like him may be intellectuals, but they are not sissies—give them half a chance and you'll discover them to be just as virile as your average businessman, politician, or Hemingway.

Most significantly, however, it seems to be exclusion from the male-dominated "public" world that plays such a big part in firing Herzog up intellectually: big ideas and "significant questions" are the payoff for accepting powerlessness.

Sometimes, indeed, *Herzog* seems to have been written almost as a textbook on sublimation. For (and perhaps this is why a book featuring comic arguments with Heidegger and Nietzsche could have remained on the *New York Times* best-seller list for so many months), at its deepest level the novel examines the therapeutic options available to a civilized man when his "sexual powers" have been "damaged" by a cheating wife and when unthinkable murder has leaped into his heart.

After his breakup with Madeleine, Herzog feels like "a convalescent" because he senses that he has lost the "ability to attract women." As a restorative he takes up with one of his night-school students—Ramona Donsella. Ramona is a "sexual professional (or priestess)," a "true sack artist" who keeps copies of Norman O. Brown's books on her bedside table. Ramona seems to specialize in sexual recuperation. She provides all the conventional preliminaries—wine, good food, exotic music—and her bedroom act includes black lace and lingerie and "spike-heeled shoes, three inches high" on which she makes her entrances.

Generally, "for the most high-minded reasons," Ramona carries on "like one of those broads in a girlie magazine." But this turns out to be all too much for Herzog. Ramona wants him "to go the whole hog," but Herzog does not want to turn himself into "a petit-bourgeois Dionysian." For Herzog, the erotic life, as directed by Ramona, represents a form of "liberation" that is all too extreme. He can neither restore himself nor get back at Madeleine by giving himself over to the "Mystical Body."

For a man in Herzog's position, from sex there is really nowhere to go but violence. Throughout the novel, Herzog sporadically imagines all kinds of pains and tortures for Madeleine and Gersbach. During one of his sessions of "self-analysis," he gives himself over to a fantasy of revenge.

> What if he had knocked her down, clutched her hair, dragged her screaming and fighting around the room, flogged her until her buttocks bled. What if he had! He should have torn her clothes, ripped off her necklace, brought his fists down on her head.

But the scenario ends with a whimper. "He rejected this mental violence, sighing. He was afraid he was really given in secret to this sort of brutality." Like Joseph in *Dangling Man,* Herzog does not "like to think what we are governed by" (*Dangling Man*), and feeling that "his rage is so great and deep, so murderous, bloody, positively rapturous, that his arms and fingers ache to strangle them [Madeleine and Gersbach]," Herzog concludes that it is a good thing that the civilized forces of "social organization" exist to keep him in check.

It does indeed seem to be a good thing, when, two-thirds into the novel Herzog sets off from New York for Chicago with the intention of murdering Madeleine and Gersbach. Herzog's decision to take such drastic action is precipitated by an ugly scene that he witnesses in a New York courtroom.

Herzog is hanging around in the courts waiting to see his divorce lawyer, Simkin. Simkin is late, and Herzog wanders into a nearby courtroom. His attention is soon riveted by a gruesome case of child murder that is being tried. The background of the murderess is desperate. She is epileptic, crippled, poverty-stricken, and had been sexually abused as a child. Her lover, indifferent and senseless, watched while she battered her child to death. Herzog is sickened by what he hears, doubly so, for the trial has a personal significance for him that is not immediately apparent. Early in the novel, Herzog has learned that Madeleine and Gersbach have locked his daughter, Junie, in their car; apparently so that they could get on with a lover's tiff in peace. The child murder thus recalls for Herzog the cruelty to his own child. For the reader, and presumably for Herzog's unconscious, there are even more points of reference. The mother of the murdered child is a "redheaded woman" with a "ruddy face," something that recalls Valentine Gersbach's flaming red hair. She also wears an orthopedic boot, reinforcing the association with Gersbach, who has only one good leg. Of the witnesses for the prosecution, one is a "salesman in the storm-window business." Our association must be with Herzog erecting storm windows in his backyard immediately prior to Madeleine's dismissing him from their house. The triangle of Herzog's personal drama is thus exaggerated and repeated in the courtroom. The defendants are, projectively, Madeleine and Gersbach; the prosecuting witness, Herzog himself.

When he gets to Chicago, Herzog retrieves his father's old handgun from his stepmother's apartment and rushes off to do away with his betrayers. However, when he arrives at his old house, Herzog first sights Gersbach through a window, tenderly bathing little Junie. To his own astonishment, he is moved rather than incensed. When his daughter is safely out of the bathroom, Herzog has a chance to fire but he merely turns away.

> There were two bullets in the chamber. . . . But they would stay there. Herzog clearly recognized that. Very softly he stepped down from his perch. . . . He saw his child in the kitchen, looking up at Mady . . . and he edged through the gate into the alley. Firing this pistol was nothing but a thought.

For Herzog, violence is no more the way to quiet his inner rage than is wild sexual activity the way to restore his sexual powers.

What can this civilized Herzog do to help resolve his crisis? He can, and does, "change it all into language." Language is Herzog's abundant compensation. In a central passage in the novel, Herzog attempts to explain to his friend Lucas Asphalter just why he has been expending so much energy on writing mental letters.

> Still, what can thoughtful people and humanists do but struggle toward suitable words? Take me, for instance. I've been writing letters helter-skelter in all directions. More words. I go after reality with language. Perhaps I'd like to change it all into language, to force Madeleine and Gersbach to have a *Conscience.* There's a word for you. I must be trying to keep tight the tensions without which human beings can no longer be called human. If they don't suffer they've gotten away from me. And I've filled the world with letters to prevent their escape. I want them in human form, and so I conjure up a whole environment and catch them in the middle. I put my whole heart into these constructions. But they are constructions.

Madeleine and Gersbach changed into language become altogether more manageable. Herzog does not say so, but it seems as if finding "suitable words" to describe his situation does much more to restore his potency than either Ramona's nightclub act or his fooling around with guns. Herzog's manic correspondence with all and sundry is both an expression of his deepest frustrations and an antidote to his suffering.

Unlike the heroes who precede him, Herzog does not "agonize" so much as use his agony to light wonderful intellectual fires; fires that lend an aura of brilliance to the novel. But, almost perversely, we know that a Herzog restored to full "health" will also be a less vitally intellectual Herzog. The novel, in fact, must end when Herzog is "released" from his obsession with Madeleine, for he is bound to be simultaneously released from his need to "fill the world with letters." And, indeed, when Herzog does finally, joyously, feel that his "servitude" to Madeleine is over, that his heart is "released from its grisly heaviness and frustration," he soon discovers that he has no further need to engage in intellectual conflicts with philosophers, writers, and politicians.

At the end of the novel, Herzog repairs to his country house in Ludeyville—a parodic Romantic retreat, a Yeatsian tower that Herzog ironically refers to as "Herzog's Folly." Here he wanders around his twenty acres of hillside and woodlot, moving closer and closer toward the deep internal silence that he has been longing for. Finally, alone in his garden, feeling *"satisfied to be, to be just as it is willed, and for as long as [he] may remain in occupancy,"* Herzog discovers that he has "no messages for anyone. Nothing. Not a single word."

In Bellow's early novels, we remain mired in the problems of heroes who are caught between a desire for order and a fear of limitation, and who seem inordinately pained by their need to repress their sexual and aggressive instincts. But in *Herzog,* Bellow allows his hero to take off from these problems: they are the rocket fuel but they do not determine where the rocket will go. From *Herzog* onward, thanks to their ability to change reality into language—or any kind of sophisticated internal musing—Bellow's heroes no longer struggle with the fact that they are being paralyzed, bullied, cheated, repressed, oppressed, or in some vital way restricted either by an individual, a group of individuals, or society as a whole. Instead they seem almost grateful to find themselves in the state of being that they know catapults them into higher states of mind. Bellow's "late" heroes give up on trying to solve the insoluble problems of their existence. However, when the troubled Bellovian hero is no longer really troubled, the reader tends to sit back and watch the intellectual show. It is a wonderful show, but its effect is to distance rather than engage us with the novel.

Chronology

1915	Born July 10 in Montreal, Canada, the fourth child of Abraham Bellow and Liza Gordon Bellow.
1924	Family moves to Chicago.
1933	Graduates from Tuley High School and enters University of Chicago.
1935	Transfers to Northwestern University.
1937	B.A. from Northwestern.
1941	"Two Morning Monologues," first publication.
1942	"The Mexican General."
1944	*Dangling Man,* first novel.
1947	*The Victim.*
1948	Guggenheim Fellowship.
1949	"Sermon of Dr. Pep."
1951	"Looking for Mr. Green"; "By the Rock Wall"; "Address by Gooley MacDowell to the Hasbeens Club of Chicago."
1952	National Institute of Arts and Letters Award.
1953	*The Adventures of Augie March;* National Book Award; translates Isaac Bashevis Singer's "Gimpel the Fool" from the Yiddish.
1955	"A Father-to-Be"; Guggenheim Fellowship.
1956	*Seize the Day;* "The Gonzaga Manuscripts."
1958	"Leaving the Yellow House"; Ford Foundation grant.
1959	*Henderson the Rain King.*
1960–62	Coedits *The Noble Savage;* Friends of Literature Fiction Award.
1962	Honorary Doctor of Letters, Northwestern University; joins Committee on Social Thought at the University of Chicago.
1963	Edits *Great Jewish Short Stories;* Honorary Doctor of Letters, Bard College.

1964   *Herzog;* James L. Dow Award; National Book Award; Fomentor Award; *The Last Analysis* opens on Broadway.

1965   International Prize for *Herzog;* three one-act plays: "Out from Under," "Orange Souffle," "A Wen."

1967   "The Old System"; reports on the Six-Day War for Newsday magazine.

1968   *Mosby's Memoirs and Other Stories;* Jewish Heritage Award from B'nai B'rith; French *Croix de Chevalier des Arts et Lettres.*

1970   *Mr. Sammler's Planet.*

1971   National Book Award for *Mr. Sammler's Planet.*

1974   "Zetland: By a Character Witness."

1975   *Humboldt's Gift.*

1976   *To Jerusalem and Back: A Personal Account;* Nobel Prize for Literature.

1978   "A Silver Dish."

1982   *The Dean's December.*

1984   *Him with His Foot in His Mouth and Other Stories.*

1987   *More Die of Heartbreak.*

Contributors

HAROLD BLOOM, Sterling Professor of the Humanities at Yale University, is the author of *The Anxiety of Influence*, *Poetry and Repression*, and many other volumes of literary criticism. His forthcoming study, *Freud: Transference and Authority*, attempts a full-scale reading of all of Freud's major writings. A MacArthur Prize Fellow, he is general editor of five series of literary criticism published by Chelsea House. During 1987–88, he served as Charles Eliot Norton Professor of Poetry at Harvard University.

TONY TANNER is a lecturer in English at Cambridge University. His books include *The Reign of Wonder* and *City of Words*.

GABRIEL JOSIPOVICI is a Reader in English at Sussex University. In addition to his considerable output of fiction, his critical works are *The Word and the Book*, *The Lessons of Modernism: Selected Reviews, 1977–1982*, and *Writing and the Body*.

SARAH BLACHER COHEN is Professor of English at SUNY at Albany. She is the editor of *Comic Relief: Humor in Contemporary American Literature*, and the author of *Saul Bellow's Enigmatic Laughter* and *From Hester Street to Hollywood: The Jewish American Stage and Screen*.

RICHARD POIRIER is Professor of English at Rutgers University. An editor of *Partisan Review* from 1963–73, he has written on James, Mailer, and Frost. Among his many familiar books on American literature are *The Performing Self*, *A World Elsewhere*, and most recently *The Renewal of Literature: Emersonian Reflections*.

DANIEL FUCHS teaches in the English Department at CUNY at Staten

Island. He has written *Vision and Revision: The Comic Spirit of Wallace Stevens* and numerous articles on Saul Bellow.

ADA AHARONI is the author of *The Second Exodus*.

JONATHAN WILSON, author of *On Bellow's Planet: Readings from the Dark Side*, is Professor of English at Tufts University.

Bibliography

Axthelm, Peter M. *The Modern Confessional Novel*. New Haven and London: Yale University Press, 1967.

Bakker, Jan. *Fiction as Survival Strategy: A Comparative Study of the Major Works of Ernest Hemingway and Saul Bellow*. Amsterdam: Rodopi, 1983. Published as volume 37 of the *Costerus* (n.s.).

Boyers, Robert. "Literature and Culture: An Interview with Saul Bellow." *Salmagundi* 30 (1975): 6–23.

Bradbury, Malcolm. *Saul Bellow*. New York: Methuen, 1982.

Braham, Jeanne. *A Sort of Columbus: The American Voyages of Saul Bellow's Fiction*. Athens: University of Georgia Press, 1984.

Chavkin, Allan. "Bellow's Alternative to the Wasteland: Romantic Theme and Form in *Herzog*." *Studies in the Novel* 2 (1979): 326–37.

Clayton, John Jacob. *Saul Bellow: In Defense of Man*. 2d ed. Bloomington: Indiana University Press, 1979.

Cohen, Sarah Blacher. *Saul Bellow's Enigmatic Laughter*. Urbana: University of Illinois Press, 1974.

Critique: Studies in Modern Fiction 7 and 9. Special Saul Bellow issues.

Dutton, Robert R. *Saul Bellow*. Rev. ed. Boston: Twayne, 1982.

———. *Saul Bellow: A Critical Essay*. Grand Rapids, Mich.: Eerdmans, 1967.

Eisinger, Chester E. "Saul Bellow: Love and Identity." *Accent* 18 (1958): 179–203.

Elgin, Don D. "Order Out of Chaos: Bellow's Use of the Picaresque in *Herzog*." *Saul Bellow Journal* 3, no. 2 (Spring/Summer 1984): 13–22.

Elliot, George. "Hurtsog, Hairtsog, Heart's Hog?" *The Nation* 199 (1964): 252–54.

Finkelstein, Sidney. *Existentialism and Alienation in American Literature*. New York: International Publishers, 1965.

Fuchs, Daniel. *Saul Bellow: Vision and Revision*. Durham, N.C.: Duke University Press, 1984.

Galloway, David. *The Absurd Hero in American Fiction: Updike, Styron, Bellow and Salinger*. Austin: University of Texas Press, 1966.

———. "Moses-Bloom-Herzog: Bellow's Everyman." *The Southern Review* 2 (1966): 61–76.

Goldman, Liela H. *Saul Bellow's Moral Vision: A Study of the Jewish Experience*. New York: Irvington Publishers, 1983.

Guttman, Allen. "Saul Bellow's Humane Comedy." In *Comic Relief: Humor in Contemporary American Literature,* edited by Sarah Blacher Cohen, 127–51. Urbana: University of Illinois Press, 1978.

Harper, Howard M., Jr. *Desperate Faith: A Study of Bellow, Salinger, Mailer, Baldwin, and Updike.* Chapel Hill: The University of North Carolina Press, 1967.

Harris, Mark. *Saul Bellow: Drumlin Woodchuck.* Athens: University of Georgia Press, 1980.

Hassan, Ihab H. *Radical Innocence: Studies in the Contemporary American Novel.* Princeton: Princeton University Press, 1961.

Hoffman, Michael J. "From Cohn to Herzog." *Yale Review* 58 (1969): 342–58.

Howe, Irving. "Odysseus, Flat on His Back." *The New Republic* 151 (September 19, 1964): 21-26.

———, ed. *Saul Bellow:* Herzog, *Text and Criticism.* New York: Viking, 1976.

Hyman, Stanley Edgar. "Saul Bellow's Glittering Eye." *The New Leader* 47 (September 28, 1964): 16–17.

Keegan, Robert. *The Sweeter Welcome: Voices for a Vision of Affirmation, Bellow, Malamud, and Martin Buber.* Needham Heights, Mass.: Humanitas Press, 1976.

Kemnitz, Charles. "Narration and Consciousness in *Herzog.*" *Saul Bellow Journal* 1, no. 2 (Spring/Summer 1982): 1–6.

Lemco, Gary. "Bellow's Herzog: A Flight of the Heart." *Saul Bellow Journal* 3, no. 1 (Fall/Winter 1983): 38–46.

Lercangee, Francine. *Saul Bellow, A Bibliography of Secondary Sources.* Brussels: Center for American Studies, 1977.

McCadden, Joseph F. *The Flight from Women in the Fiction of Saul Bellow.* Lanham, Md.: University Press of America, 1980.

Mailer, Norman. "Modes and Mutations: Quick Comments on the Modern American Novel." *Commentary* 41, no. 3 (March 1966): 37–40.

Malin, Irving. *Saul Bellow's Fiction.* Carbondale: Southern Illinois University Press, 1969.

———, ed. *Saul Bellow and the Critics.* New York: University Press, 1967.

Markos, Donald. "The Humanist of Saul Bellow." Ph.D. diss., University of Illinois, 1966.

Maurocordato, Alexandre. *Les quatres dimensions du* Herzog *de Saul Bellow.* Paris: Lettres Modernes, 1969.

Modern Fiction Studies 25 (Spring 1979). Special Saul Bellow issue.

Nassar, Joseph M. "The World Within: Image Clusters in *Herzog.*" *Saul Bellow Journal* 2, no. 2 (Spring/Summer 1983): 24–29.

Nault, Marianne. *Saul Bellow: His Work and His Critics: An Annotated International Bibliography.* New York: Garland, 1977.

Newman, Judith A. *Saul Bellow and History.* London: Macmillan, 1984.

Noreen, Robert G. *Saul Bellow: A Reference Guide.* Boston: G. K. Hall, 1978.

Notes on Modern American Literature 2, no. 4 (1978). Special Saul Bellow issue.

Opdahl, Keith Michael. *The Novels of Saul Bellow: An Introduction.* University Park: Pennsylvania State University Press, 1967.

Poirier, Richard. "Bellows to Herzog." *Partisan Review* 32 (1965): 264–71.

Porter, Gilbert M. *Whence the Power? The Artistry and Humanity of Saul Bellow.* Columbia: University of Missouri Press, 1974.

Rodrigues, Eusebio L. *Quest for the Human: An Exploration of Saul Bellow's Fiction*. Lewisburg, Pa.: Bucknell University Press, 1981.

Rovit, Earl. *Saul Bellow*. University of Minnesota Pamphlet on American Writers, no. 65. Minneapolis: University of Minnesota Press, 1967.

———, ed. *Saul Bellow: A Collection of Critical Essays*. Englewood Cliffs, N.J.: Prentice-Hall, 1975.

Russ, Joanna. "What Can A Heroine Do?" In *Images of Women in Fiction*, edited by Susan Koppelman Cornillon. Bowling Green, Ohio: Bowling Green University Press, 1972.

Samuel, Maurice. "My Friend, the Late Moses Herzog." *Midstream* 12, no. 4 (1966): 3–25.

Saul Bellow Journal. 1982—.

Saul Bellow Newsletter. Detroit, Mich.: Wayne State University, 1981.

Scheer-Schazler, Brigitte. *Saul Bellow*. New York: Ungar, 1972.

Schraepen, Edmond, ed. *Saul Bellow and His Work*. Brussels: Centrum voor taal- en literatuurwetenschap, Vrije Universiteit, 1978.

Schulz, Max F. *Radical Sophistication: Studies in Contemporary Jewish American Novelists*. Athens: Ohio University Press, 1969.

Scott, Nathan A. "The Bias of Comedy and the Narrow Escape into Faith." *The Christian Scholar* 44 (1961): 9–39.

———. *Three American Moralists: Mailer, Bellow, Trilling*. Notre Dame, Ind.: The University of Notre Dame Press, 1973.

Shulman, Robert. "The Style of Bellow's Comedy." *PMLA* 83 (1968): 109–17.

Studies in American Jewish Literature 3, no. 1 (Spring 1977). Special Saul Bellow issue.

Studies in American Jewish Literature. Special issue number 3, 1983.

Studies in the Literary Imagination 17, no. 2 (Fall 1984).

Tanner, Tony. *City of Words: American Fiction 1950–1970*. New York: Harper & Row, 1971.

———. "The Flight from Monologue." *Encounter* 24, no. 2 (February 1965): 58–70.

———. *Saul Bellow*. Writers and Critics, no. 50. Edinburgh: Oliver & Boyd, 1965.

Trachtenberg, Stanley, ed. *Critical Essays on Saul Bellow*. Boston: G. K. Hall, 1979.

Vinoda and Shiv Kumar. *Saul Bellow: A Symposium on the Jewish Heritage*. Hyderabad, India: Nachson Books, 1983.

Vogel, Dan. "Saul Bellow's Vision Beyond Absurdity: Jewishness in *Herzog*." *Tradition* 9, no. 4 (1960): 65–79.

Werner, Craig Hansen. *Paradoxical Resolutions: American Fiction Since James Joyce*. Urbana: University of Illinois Press, 1982.

Wilson, Jonathan. *On Bellow's Planet: Readings from the Dark Side*. London and Toronto: Associated University Presses, 1985.

Wisse, Ruth R. *The Schlemiel as Modern Hero*. Chicago: The University of Chicago Press, 1971.

Yiddish 3, no. 3 (1978) and 4, no. 1 (1979).

Acknowledgments

"The Prisoner of Perception" by Tony Tanner from *Saul Bellow* by Tony Tanner, © 1965 by Tony Tanner. Reprinted by permission of the author and Barnes & Noble Books, Totowa, New Jersey.

"*Herzog*: Freedom and Wit" by Gabriel Josipovici from *The World and the Book* by Gabriel Josipovici, © 1971, 1979 by Gabriel Josipovici. Reprinted by permission of Macmillan Press, London and Basingstoke, and Stanford University Press.

"That Suffering Joker" by Sarah Blacher Cohen from *Saul Bellow's Enigmatic Laughter* by Sarah Blacher Cohen, © 1974 by Sarah Blacher Cohen. Reprinted by permission of the author.

"Herzog, or, Bellow in Trouble" by Richard Poirier from *Saul Bellow: A Collection of Critical Essays,* edited by Earl Rovit, © 1975 by Prentice-Hall, Inc., Englewood Cliffs, New Jersey. Reprinted by permission.

"Bellow and Freud" by Daniel Fuchs from *Studies in the Literary Imagination* 17, no. 2 (Fall 1984), © 1984 by the Department of English, Georgia State University. Reprinted by permission.

"Women in Saul Bellow's Novels" by Ada Aharoni from *Studies in American Jewish Literature,* no. 3, edited by Daniel Walden, © 1983 by *Studies in American Jewish Literature*. Reprinted by permission of the State University of New York Press.

"*Herzog*: A Reading from the Dark Side" (originally entitled "*Herzog*") by Jonathan Wilson from *On Bellow's Planet: Readings from the Dark Side* by Jonathan Wilson, © 1985 by Associated University Presses, Inc. Reprinted by permission of Associated University Presses, Inc.

Index

Adams, Henry, 68
"Address by Gooley MacDowell to the Hasbeens Club of Chicago" (Bellow), 35
Adventures of Augie March, The (Bellow), 1, 5, 68, 71, 114; *Herzog* compared to, 61; transcendentalism in, 2–3
Aestheticism, Bellow and, 5
Alienation: Bellow and, 63–64, 65, 68, 70–71; in *Herzog*, 12
Allusion, Moses Herzog and use of, 58–60
American Dream, An (Mailer), 44
American literature, Bellow on, 116
Antimodernist, Bellow as, 5–6, 74
Art, Freud and, 87
Asphalter, Lucas, 28–29, 49, 115, 119

Beck, Evelyn Torton, 106
Bellow, Saul: and aestheticism, 5; and alienation, 63–64, 65, 68, 70–71; on American literature, 116; as antimodernist, 5–6, 74; Buber's influence on, 97; in character of Moses Herzog, 6, 33–34, 68; as comic writer, 64–65, 93; compared to Mailer, 1, 63; compared to Nabokov, 6; compared to Perelman, 71; compared to Svevo, 5–6; compared to Swift, 22; compared to Twain, 7; critical opinion of, 1; and Flaubert, 5; and Freudian psy-

chology, 6; Freud's influence on, 73–76, 77–78, 79–80, 81, 85–86, 87–88, 90–94; Fromm's influence on, 81–83; on *Herzog*, 1, 39, 40–41, 112; as humanist, 79, 85, 91; as Jewish writer, 65, 91; on Judaism, 85; opposition to Freud, 73–74, 76, 77–78, 79, 81, 83, 84–85, 86–87, 88, 90, 91, 92–93, 94; as polemicist, 5–7; as recipient of Nobel Prize for Literature, 102; and religion, 81, 82; as sentimentalist, 6; on the unconscious, 75–76; Whitman's influence on, 2; and women, 5, 6, 95
Bellow's novels: characterization in, 1–2, 120; women as characters in, 95–97, 98–101, 102–7
"Bernard Malamud and the Jewish Literary Tradition" (Rovit), 60
"Bias of Comedy and the Narrow Escape into Faith, The" (Scott), 40
Blake, William, 6
Bradbury, Malcolm, 61
Brothers Karamazov, The (Dostoevsky), 84–85, 87, 115
Buber, Martin, influence on Bellow, 97

Catholic Church, Moses Herzog and the, 53–54
Citrine, Charlie *(Humboldt's Gift)*, 4–5, 7, 81, 82, 89, 90